Porcelain Travels
Humor, Horror and Revelation
in, on and around
Toilets, Tubs and Showers

Matthew Félix

Porcelain Travels:
Humor, Horror and Revelation in, on and around Toilets, Tubs and Showers
by Matthew Félix

Published by solificatio

2018 Trade Paperback Edition

"A Turkish Bath in Morocco" and "The Dunes" originally published
in *With Open Arms: Short Stories of Misadventures in Morocco* also by
Matthew Félix

matthewfelix.com

ISBN-10: 0-9977619-2-X
ISBN-13: 978-0-9977619-2-4

CONTENTS

1 IT AIN'T OVER, TILL IT'S…

It was my first trip to Morocco, and I had just arrived in Tangier.

It had been an absolute nightmare.

I'd been mobbed. I'd been harassed. I'd been called racist and then Jewish, by an ignorant thug oblivious to the irony. After I rid myself of him, another tout jumped at me from inside a dark stairwell. We engaged in a nerve-wracking exchange of lies in not one but two languages, during which I had very real reason to fear being physically assaulted. That fear increased exponentially when I turned my back on my would-be assailant to climb a flight of stairs. It was a high-stakes gamble, but it paid off. At the top of the stairs, at long last, I checked into a hotel.

My room was rough around the edges, but it still had some of its original colonial charm: high ceilings, crown molding, and two sets of doors that opened onto small balconies overlooking the bustling square below. The room had a little sink, too, for washing up.

What it did not have was a bathroom.

I had already had the shit metaphorically scared out of me. No surprise that I now had similar, albeit more literal needs. Addressing them entailed a walk down the hall.

It didn't seem right. Having only just found refuge from a violent barrage of annoyances and dangers, I already had to leave it behind? I'd barely caught my breath. All I wanted to do was lock myself inside my room ... for days.

But Nature called.

After hiding my passport and checking twice that I'd locked the door, I walked down the musty, dimly lit hallway. The gentlemanly hotel manager and a group of young male prostitutes (I didn't learn their vocation until later) were sitting in the lobby watching an important soccer match. The sound of cheering fans and the voice of a high-strung announcer echoed through the corridor. Several doors down, almost at the end of the hall, I found the bathroom.

Given my extreme fatigue, the idea of squatting over a dirty, odorous hole was even less appealing than it might have been were I in better shape emotionally and physically. Not that it mattered. I wasn't going to go look for another hotel. No way in hell was I setting foot back in those godforsaken alleys. Not tonight, anyway.

It could have been worse. It was dingy, but a bottle of disinfectant suggested it had been cleaned within recent memory. And it was hardly the first time I'd used a Turkish toilet.

I looked around. The bathroom door had a translucent windowpane, ostensibly so people could tell whether the toilet was in use. Like tooth enamel tarnished by excessive coffee and cigarettes, walls that had once been white had long since yellowed. Did people smoke in here? If so, more overpowering odors snuffed out any lingering traces of tobacco.

I peered into the black hole, shuddering at the thought of the unspeakable secrets hidden in its depths. At the same time, I contemplated my own secret. I couldn't wait much longer to share it.

Doing so was going to be tricky. Black holes suck things in and swallow them. The only thing between me and oblivion was the white porcelain basin that surrounded the hole. On each side of the basin were raised areas with flat tops. I carefully positioned my right foot on one and my left on the other. It was imperative they not slip.

I pulled down my pants and assumed the position.

Already my legs were wobbling. I hoped they would hold up.

Although I did have to stand up once to give my fatiguing thighs a brief reprieve, my business was conducted with welcome celerity. There were no long, drawn-out negotiations, no unpleasant sticking points, nothing to keep the deal from going through.

Until I went to close the transaction.

Perhaps not everything was in place, after all.

Bathroom cleaner. A used-up brush. A blue plastic pail next to a spigot in the wall.

Where was the toilet paper?

I should have known. Unfortunately, I'd been shell-shocked from my arrival and hadn't planned on making a trek to the bathroom. Even if I had, in my post-traumatic stupor, it probably wouldn't have occurred to me to grab my spare roll of toilet paper.

"Shit," I exclaimed, immediately realizing the irony. I broke into solitary, delusional laughter. This could not be happening. After everything I'd endured, my nightmarish welcome to Morocco still was not over? Hadn't all that come to an end the moment I crossed the threshold of the hotel, a refugee finally safe and sound in a compassionate, hospitable land?

Apparently not.

Yet another cultural experience awaited before I could call it a day, one more rite of passage. And this one wasn't going to be pretty.

Unless I wanted to squat there all night, I had to overcome my hesitation. I had to transcend my disbelief. I had to put the little pail under the spigot and turn on the water.

Sound filled the room, water streaming into plastic, the tone changing as the water level rose. The little pail shook as though overwhelmed. I turned the water off.

Again, I hesitated. Once more, I deliberated.

I was well aware that toilet paper was a luxury, that people around the world routinely had no choice but to use their hands after relieving themselves. I never had. Ideally, I never would. Call me privileged, call me a coward, I did not want to stick my hand into my own feces.

Was there another way around it?

I decided to try.

If my legs had tired quickly before, the contortions to which I was about to subject my body now threatened to push them over their limit. It was, after all, a delicate operation. My feet could not move from their porcelain pedestals. I needed to keep my pants taut around my ankles, so they didn't come into contact with the filthy basin. If I didn't want to get my clothes or feet wet, I had to stick my butt as far away from my body as possible, without losing balance. I'm sure there's a name for the yoga pose I was suddenly struggling to assume, but it wasn't one I'd ever seen in class.

Once I'd achieved the desired posture, I didn't have a second to lose. I poured the water between my buttocks, hoping it would do the job on its own.

What it did instead was cascade down my legs, spilling all over my pants and splattering onto the floor.

I shot up, my legs on the verge of collapse. I was angry. I was frustrated. I might have even been a little humiliated.

All I wanted was to go to bed. The thought of making a mad dash to the port and catching a ferry back to Spain crossed my mind. If the last one of the day had already departed, maybe I'd swim.

The bathroom had no ventilation. The longer I stayed inside, the stuffier it got. Sweat was falling from my forehead in fully formed drops. I had to get this over and done with. Fast.

I squatted, stuck my butt out, and poured. Once again my legs got drenched, as did my pants. So much for the lessons I thought I'd learned from my previous attempt. My second try was as much a failure as the first.

I gave it more thought. I went over it again and again,

hoping to come up with yet another solution. All I was doing was avoiding the inevitable.

I filled the bucket with more water.

Was I really going to do this?

I looked down at the wretched hole. I wiped more sweat from my brow. I had to get out of there.

I got back into position. I stuck my hand into the water.

I stuck my hand into the darkness.

I groaned in disgust.

I would have loved to have stopped with that single gesture. Now that I'd crossed the line, however, there was no going back. I had to finish what I had started—and there was only one way to do it. More water. More bare hand.

Even worse that I was using the wrong hand. I didn't have a choice. I hadn't grown up in a culture where one hand was traditionally reserved for unclean acts, the other for social interactions. My left hand didn't have the necessary coordination, and I didn't have the time to train it. I used my right.

Later in my travels I would come to find that water can be as effective, if not more so, than toilet paper (there's a reason, after all, that bidets persist in Europe). I wasn't there yet the first time around. Suffice it to say it was a rush job: my hand may have been in it, but my heart was not.

Considerably more self-aware than a mere twenty minutes prior, I stumbled back to my room. My legs and back ached. My pants were as damp as if I'd wet them. My body was almost as bad, covered from head to toe in sweat.

Before I could close my eyes and drift off to a world where the preceding three hours had never happened, there was one last thing I had to do.

I walked over to the little sink and unwrapped a complimentary, travel-sized bar of nameless soap. It gave off a vague perfume. I proceeded to scrub my right hand until it was so red it was on the verge of bleeding. I then scrubbed it some more. When the bar of soap broke in two, I eased up. The last thing I wanted to do was break the skin.

In a few short days, after all, someone else would do that for me; they would draw blood at a stop further down the road.

My misadventures in Morocco had only just begun.

2 THE BIN AND THE BOMB

I needed a place to live in Paris.

I had interrupted an extended period of traveling in Europe to return to the U.S. for the holidays. Now I was back, and I planned to settle in Paris for a few months. I could stay with my French friend, Sophie, initially; but I didn't want to wear out my welcome.

Oddly enough, Sophie didn't have a high-speed Internet connection in her apartment. So, a couple of days after my arrival, I found myself in a café that, according to the sign on the door, offered free Internet access. I ordered an espresso, got a table next to the window, and opened my laptop.

Everything seemed to be going as planned until I discovered, per some fine print on the receipt that arrived with my coffee, that the "free" Internet access would last all of fifteen minutes. I felt duped. In order to accomplish what I needed to get done, I'd have to down an espresso every fifteen minutes for the next two or three hours. My Internet connection may not have been wired, but I sure as hell would be.

I decided to check if any other (legitimately) free wireless networks were breaching the walls of the technologically backward café. It wasn't like at home; at the time, free Wi-Fi was still much less common in Paris. But it was worth a shot.

A list of networks came up. Not only was I in luck, I was surprised. An abrupt and selfish change of heart was about to leave me considering an old archenemy my new best friend.

Along with the nauseating smell of greasy burgers, a McDonald's on the other side of the plaza was spewing out free wireless waves—one more Web to ensnare prospective customers. Or, in my case, one more ploy to recapture a sheep long ago strayed from the flock. I hadn't set foot under the Golden Arches for well over a decade. Now it was as if they'd turned upside down and were smiling back at me from my computer screen. Like an adversary who knows the battle is lost before it's begun, I did not put up a fight.

The following week saw me in McDonald's twice a day almost every day. I spent countless hours poring over housing ads, researching a never-ending list of questions about living in Paris, and keeping up on email. In no time, I was a regular.

But I wasn't lovin' it.

At first it was tough. Even during my time doing high-school theater, I'd never been subjected to such bright, overpowering lights. At the end of each visit, I was a little paler than at the beginning, my skin taking on the bland color of the fries drowning in the bubbling cauldrons behind the counter. Then there was the inescapable stink of food being made way too fast. It smelled greasy. It smelled fake-fresh and saccharine-sweet—though the latter seemed odd. Did they sweeten the burgers and fries? It nauseated me.

So did what I ate. After all, I couldn't sit there for hours at a time without ordering something. Looking up at the huge display over the counter, I discovered three less-than-a-euro options. One was a little package of inconceivably perfect fruit, a veritable testament to the marvels of genetic engineering. There was also a fruit-and-yogurt cup and two varieties of milkshakes.

I naively assumed the fruit-and-yogurt cup would be a healthy option. I gave it a try. It tasted as though it had nearly as much sugar as a milkshake. In that case, why bother? I might as well just have the shake.

I was in for yet another surprise. I could not process the shake. It made me weak. I don't know if it was the amount of sugar or whatever mysterious compounds might have comprised the chemical concoction (did it even contain any milk?), but my body could not metabolize it. The milkshake gave me the sugar shakes, and I had trouble focusing—to the point of rendering me unable to get any work done. It was as if the neurons in my brain lost the ability to send and receive impulses, mired as they were in synthetic vanilla goo. How did people drink these things on a regular basis? In addition to having a warning label, they needed to be served with a side of insulin and a syringe.

After a week of searching, I appeared to have found a place to live. To be sure, I needed to see it in person. I set up an appointment and, the next day, I went to check out the apartment.

Stéphane met me at the metro station and whisked me off to his place, just a couple of minutes away. In order to see it, it was necessary to climb seven flights of stairs. The building was an old, grandiose Haussmann in an upscale neighborhood. I commented that it seemed odd there wasn't an elevator.

"There is," Stéphane responded, before bounding out of sight, "we just don't get to use it."

The apartment was a *chambre de bonne*, or service room, which was essentially where "the help" lived way back when. More than welcome in the homes of their employers when cooking or cleaning, at all other times apparently the servants were to remain out of sight. That explained why, even though the building did in fact have an elevator, it didn't go to the top floor—where the service rooms were located. The servants didn't even have off-hour access to the main entrance. Instead, they were expected to use a separate, discreet door a few feet away, the same one through which the trash was dragged in and out.

So much for *fraternité, égalité,* and *liberté.*

Stéphane vaulted up each flight as he had countless times before, not only his years of experience but the long legs on his tall, lanky frame affording him a considerable advantage over me. Not that I wished him any ill will, but I was almost relieved when I found him panting at the top of the stairs. My relief was short-lived. I was soon seeing not one but several Stéphanes, each moving about like crystals in a kaleidoscope.

I sat down and put my head between my knees. For a moment I was back in the only session of Bikram yoga I had ever dared attend, reliving the alarming instant I realized that—although I was watching him, and he was still talking—I no longer heard anything the instructor in the classroom-cum-sauna was saying. "This must be what it feels like before you pass out," it occurred to me. Every drop of blood in my body had drained below my waist. If I didn't sit down that very instant, it would be lights out.

"It's harder if you stop part way up," Stéphane offered. I barely nodded, like a coma patient who can only communicate by moving his big toe.

Stéphane and his girlfriend, a Chilean woman named María, were getting ready to spend a few months traveling around South America, which was why they were subletting their apartment. When we opened the door, María was there to greet us. There was, after all, no other place for her to be.

I have no idea how it was possible for two adults to cohabitate in such confined quarters. Prisoners sharing a cell have more room to move around. Astronauts in space stations have more privacy. Even conjoined twins live more separate lives than Stéphane and María at home together.

"Well, here it is," Stéphane proclaimed, in a timid statement of the obvious. He seemed nervous.

"Here it is!" I echoed, not sure what else to say. I also forced a smile, hoping to disguise my shock and dismay.

"Well, ah," Stéphane began, looking around as though trying to figure out where to start, "there's the futon, which folds out into a bed. And the wood plank hanging from the chain can be put up against the wall, when you're not using it as a table."

He proceeded to give me a demonstration. I, however, was distracted. Looking beyond the retractable table, through a large window I beheld an unobstructed, top-to-bottom view of the Eiffel Tower. It was breathtaking. Other than from open spaces like the Trocadéro or the Champs de Mars, I wouldn't have thought such a view was even possible.

"That's the TV," Stéphane continued, making yet another statement of the obvious. A large screen hung on an adjustable arm sticking out of the wall. Couldn't miss it.

"And there's the Internet connection," he concluded.

I looked down at the floor, where a blinking black box sat atop a tangled nest of wires.

"The sink's in there," María interjected, motioning to a minuscule alcove off the main room. It was about as big as one of those old ironing-board closets.

"Yeah, and the hotplate and microwave," added Stéphane. Apparently, the alcove served as the kitchen. "It's really, really important you turn off the gas whenever you're done using the hotplate."

"Butane tanks aren't allowed in apartments anymore," María explained, "because there have been some explosions. But we don't have any other way to cook."

It made perfect sense. If they couldn't cook, they couldn't eat, and they would die. Without cooking, death was certain; death by butane-tank explosion, on the other hand, was merely a possibility. Like any prudent, rational thinkers, they had chosen the less risky option.

I took a closer look. On the shelf under the microwave, there was a small butane tank. Ironically, other than the fact it was blue, it looked just like one of those stereotypical bowling-ball bombs in old cartoons. A hose ran behind some shelves, connecting the tank to a two-burner camping stove, which Stéphane had referred to as the hotplate. That was where I would be doing my cooking; assuming, of course, that I, myself, wasn't burnt to a crisp in yet another unfortunate, newsworthy mishap.

"That's why you also have to make sure you always open the window when you're cooking," cautioned Stéphane, while showing me how to raise the small, four-paned window over the camping stove.

"And please don't remove the piece of paper. The windowpane is broken on the other side, and the paper keeps it in place," he added.

I looked at the paper. It featured a huge set of lips that had benefited from a reparation, volumizing, and anti-aging regimen developed by a Parisian laboratory. I made a mental note never to remove the paper from the window. Wouldn't want to hurt those pretty lips—especially not after all the work that had gone into them.

Returning my attention to whether I was up for the dangers of living with a potential bomb, not to mention the every bit as sinister threat of a gas leak lulling me into a permanent slumber, María deftly changed the subject.

"The bathroom!" she said.

"Oh yeah!" responded Stéphane with a smile, as though he couldn't believe he hadn't thought of it sooner. "Come on."

We stepped back out into the hallway. As we did, Stéphane insisted it was paramount I always carry the key with me whenever I left the room, since the door locked automatically. I made another mental note, adding it to the ones about the gas and the lips.

We walked to the end of the hall, where Stéphane opened a narrow door that, from the outside, appeared to be a closet. And in a sense, it was. I found myself presented with the very embodiment of a "water closet." Besides a tall window, there was room for nothing in the little chamber other than a toilet and the brush used to clean it.

There were actually two water closets—one at each end of the hall. They were shared with the neighbors, creatures of the night who were few in number and rarely seen.

"As you can tell, it's clean. The neighbors are very

respectful," María pointed out, in case I hadn't noticed. I had. But my mind had already moved onto something else.

As elsewhere in my travels, "water closet" was not to be confused with the more comprehensive term "bathroom." There was neither a sink nor a tub or shower in the little room. Where did Stéphane and María bathe, I wondered. The answer would prove to be an ingenious—albeit unorthodox—setup back in the kitchen alcove.

Hanging from the ceiling were two shower curtains I had overlooked initially, no doubt while wondering if the benefits of renting the apartment outweighed the risk of dying in it. Stéphane explained the role the curtains played in maintaining his and María's personal hygiene.

"It's easier if you just shower at the pool," he began, "but, when you want to shower here, first you have to put this on the floor." He motioned to an empty rubber bin that had been resting against the wall. It was the size of a laundry basket.

"Then," continued María, "you unhook the shower curtains, and let them come to rest in the bin."

Like a flight attendant describing life-saving techniques, she demonstrated the procedure.

"After that, you take this hose and hook it up to the sink. Then you turn on the water, get it to the right temperature, and take your shower," explained Stéphane. "You just have to make sure not to take too long. Otherwise the bin will overflow, and you'll have a big mess on your hands!"

I thought of the time at home when I'd failed to turn the faucet all the way off, after going to the bathroom in the middle of the night. The sink had a slow drain, and the water overflowed, flooding the bathroom floor—and seeping through my downstairs neighbor's ceiling. Earplugs had ensured I slept through it all, until my panicked landlord came pounding on my door early the next morning. A big mess, indeed.

Returning to the situation at hand, I considered the facts.

By Parisian standards, the apartment was cheap. Most other apartments I'd found were much more expensive. Still—

forgetting for a moment the whole bomb thing—was I really up to showering in a laundry basket? Although I'm normally more adaptable than just about anyone I know, that sort of felt like taking it to a new extreme. On the other hand, I wouldn't have to live with roommates. The apartment had a high-speed Internet connection and a TV. It also had that spectacular view of the Eiffel Tower.

Then, of course, there was the one factor I had been conveniently overlooking: I was out of time. No other feasible options had presented themselves, and I didn't feel comfortable extending my stay at Sophie's.

I talked the chronically codependent couple down 100 euros a month.

We had a deal.

The apartment had another disadvantage.

It wasn't heated.

Not exactly. There was a small electrical wall unit; however, Stéphane had never used it—not once during the six or seven years he had lived in the little room. I was welcome to give it a try, he offered, but he wasn't sure how well it would work—let alone if there was any danger in doing so. At the very least, he cautioned, a lot of dust would probably fly out. There was also a chance the unit would catch fire.

Rousing the heater from its nearly decade-long repose seemed about as prudent as prying the lid off a cursed ancient tomb. Inevitably, people who did that in the movies spontaneously combusted. I decided not to risk it.

The wall heater little more than a defunct relic, the only heat source was a group of water pipes running through the kitchen ceiling. When it wasn't unbearably cold outside, the water pipes helped. Unfortunately, it was January in Paris. Most of the time, it was, in fact, unbearably cold outside.

I was freezing.

I dressed in layers, starting with thermal underwear. It

quickly became clear that I needed about three more pairs of them. The clothes I had brought with me were direly insufficient.

One particularly brutal morning, looking out onto a cold, gray Parisian day, I watched as each breath I exhaled took on its own unique form. If I'd been more skilled, I might have made little rings, like the experienced pipe smokers. Questioning my ability to survive the bone-chilling cold another day, I decided to rummage through Stéphane's clothes in the hopes of finding something warmer than my own.

I discovered a very peculiar garment.

A heavy, bright-red robe with a thick trim of white, a zipper down the middle to the waist, and a pointy hood, it looked like what Santa Claus might wear if he joined the Klu Klux Klan. As I pulled it out of the closet, I couldn't possibly imagine how essential it would become for weathering what ended up being the coldest weeks of the year. I wore it almost non-stop— hood and all—every day I was at home.

If the robe came in handy while I was in my room, it was even more useful when Nature called. My tiny servant's quarters may have been cold, but they were nothing compared to the bathroom. Not only did it lack a heating source, but its window had an old, cracked frame. Any heat that might have otherwise warmed the little room made a quick and easy escape. If I had ever been one to linger on the pot, there was no danger of that now.

Unless, of course, I got stuck.

Every time I sat down on the icy toilet at the end of the hall, my Santa Klan robe bunched around my waist, I thought of a particular afternoon when I was a child.

It was a sweltering summer day. I was at my best friend's up the street, and his mom had given both of us a special treat: a chocolate pudding pop. It was delicious and, enraptured by the welcome relief of its voluptuous, ice-cold, chocolaty sweetness, I closed my eyes and wrapped my lips around it. Not a single taste bud the length and width of my tongue was denied the exquisite pleasure.

In hindsight, perhaps I was a little overzealous, since a moment later I had the rudest of awakenings: the pudding pop would not budge.

It had frozen to my lips.

A bizarre sequence of panicked gestures followed, as I desperately attempted to communicate to my friend what had happened. In no time, his mom was shoving my head under the kitchen faucet. Twisting my neck enough to make an owl wince, she tried to get my mouth upturned at just the right angle, while we waited for the running water to heat up. Her intent was to melt the pudding pop from my lips—hopefully without leaving them a bloody mess.

She was only modestly successful. The pudding pop was dislodged, but blood was shed. Indeed, anyone looking at the sink might have thought my tonsils had been removed along with the pudding pop. Shortly after, skin was grafted from my buttocks to repair the damage. I've had a pathological aversion to the expression "kiss my ass" ever since.

I thought of the pudding-pop debacle each time I sat down on the sub-freezing surface of the porcelain throne at the end of the hall. What if? I anxiously asked myself, praying I was being paranoid.

The porcelain was brutally cold. My flesh, wrapped in thermal underwear, layers of clothing, and a thick robe, was not only warm, but covered in a thin layer of perspiration. The circumstances were ripe for another pudding-pop-style calamity. A split second was all it would take for my butt cheeks to freeze to the toilet seat.

If that happened, who would come to my aid? Which of my mysterious, as yet unseen neighbors would hear—let alone find it in their hearts to respond to—my desperate cries? Even if they bothered, what would they do? Douse my ass in hot water? Place a space heater in the water closet and let me sit it out? And if I ended up needing another graft, where would the skin come from?

Too many questions for which I had no answers.

I kept moving.

There was another problem with the bathroom.

The lights kept going out.

In the interest of conserving energy, rather than a standard light switch, the water closet had one with a built-in timer. Unlike similar timers I'd seen, this one was silent. As a result, for at least the first month of my stay, I forgot about it. Over and over again. I constantly found myself taken by surprise when, while taking care of business, I was left in the dark.

I'm not sure why it took me so long to get used to the timer. Perhaps I simply wasn't accustomed to having to be so present while heeding Nature's call. The fact the timer was silent didn't help. Neither did my inability to keep an eye on it—there being nothing to keep an eye on. The inscrutable gadget offered neither an indication of how much time had expired, nor any clue as to how much remained.

Eventually, I caught on to the countdown. My solution for dealing with it, however, left much to be desired.

I essentially developed a nervous tick. I began hitting the timer button without regard to how much time had passed. My mind wandered while on the pot; I wasn't going to sit there counting the seconds. Soon I was whacking the button without even realizing it, over and over, and then some more, well on my way to developing a full-fledged obsessive-compulsive disorder. There was, however, one bright side to my madness.

The light never went out again.

I had put it off for as long as I could. I'd taken Stéphane's advice and done it at the pool. I'd skipped a day or two, before and after. But there was no longer any avoiding it: it was time for my first shower in the apartment.

I did my best to recall the instructions Stéphane and María had given me. I put the bin on the floor. I placed the shower curtains into the bin. I connected the hose to the faucet. All that remained was to adjust the water to the right temperature, get into the bin, and pull the shower curtains around me. Easy enough.

Standing naked in the alcove, I was freezing. Unfortunately, so was the water. I hadn't expected it to be a challenge; yet, try and try as I might, I could not figure out how to get the water to warm up.

At first, it was ice cold. No surprise, since I had started by turning the cold-water knob. But even when I followed it with the hot-water one, glacial melt continued to flow from the hose. I began to fear that perhaps—despite what I had been told—there wasn't any hot water to be had. Or, maybe the butane tank had already run out.

Recalling that when I had visited the apartment a week earlier I'd seen steam rising from this very sink and that the hot-water heater was electric, I took a deep breath, removed the hose from the faucet, and turned off the water.

My body now covered with goose bumps so large they looked more like goose eggs, I discovered that, when I turned the hot-water knob, nothing happened. Not a drip of water, cold or hot. My jaw dropped despite moments earlier having frozen shut. Was there really no hot water?

I paused, looking at the hotplate to my left. Worse come to worst, I could do what I had done years before in Istanbul: heat my bath water on the stove.

No. I was not going to resort to that. I had witnessed hot water coming from this very faucet. It was in there somewhere, and I was going to get it out.

With a frustrated, desperate turn evidently stronger than those before it, I twisted the knob beyond what I had thought was its stopping point. A scalding cascade rushed forth. I threw my body toward it like at a campfire on a cold winter night.

Briefly turning the water off again, I rushed to hook the hose back up to the faucet. I then made another attempt to get the water to the right temperature. Much to my chagrin, the water traveled through the hose in unpredictable bursts of hot and cold—scarcely blending. Putting myself in its range of fire would have been disastrous, no matter what came out. One instant, it was an icy-cold spray; the next, a searing-hot blast—part liquid, part steam.

Refusing to give up, I continued experimenting with the knobs until, a couple of minutes later, I succeeded in getting a more or less consistently warm stream of water flowing from the showerhead. I jumped into the bin and pulled the curtains around me.

I felt like a sandwich in a Ziploc bag. The translucent curtains clung to me. Only the force of the water was enough to separate my naked flesh from the sticky plastic. Unfortunately, since I held the showerhead in my hand and the pressure was so low, there wasn't enough water to go around. At any given time, part of my body felt enveloped in Saran Wrap—and it didn't feel good.

The discomfort of being wrapped in plastic was outweighed by the renewed ability to feel my extremities, the warm water restoring the flow of blood. But Stéphane's warning echoed in my thoughts: "You just have to make sure not to take too long!" I couldn't dillydally. Looking down, I saw that my feet were already well below the now-soapy water. Almost as soon as it had begun, the fun was over. I didn't have time to lose myself in any sort of guilty pleasure.

I gave my body a final rinse, peeled the curtains apart, and got out of the bin. The steam from the shower had warmed the room. Leaving the cellophane enclosure wasn't nearly as miserable as it might have been otherwise.

Once I'd dried off, I had to dismantle the shower. My towel wrapped around my waist, I shut off the water and pulled the hose from the faucet, allowing the water in the end of the hose to drain into the sink. The hose, however, was six or seven feet in length. Somehow I needed to empty the rest of it.

Before I knew it, I was enacting a physical comedy sketch for a few lucky tourists on the Eiffel Tower's upper decks. As I explored countless ways of positioning the hose in order to get the water out, my body stretched and strained in as many contortions as the hose itself. It was like wrestling a baby python. Innumerable containers—spices, oil and vinegar, dishwashing liquid—lined the narrow shelves of the little room, like targets in a carnival game. The writhing hose soon whacked a box of salt, sending it sailing to the floor. The box exploded in a drift of iodized white.

I was too short and the hose was too long. I raised it as high into the air as I could, but three fourths of the water remained inaccessible. No matter how I twisted and turned, I could only get a little water out. Loops of hose fell on top of me, further constricting my movement and calling that much more attention to my failure. I couldn't keep my towel around my waist. It fell to the floor.

Concluding that the sink might not be the best option, it occurred to me to drop the end of the hose into the bin instead, since it was on the ground. I then carried the rest of the hose into the main room, as far away as I could. Glancing out the window toward the Eiffel Tower, I could have sworn I saw tourists bellied over with laughter, fingers and cameras alike pointed in my direction. If my little drama went on much longer, I feared it would soon go viral.

I raised the hose again, happy when water drained into the tub. Hoping to build on my relative success, I grabbed the stool used at the makeshift desk and carefully got on top of it. That was even more effective—but I could only do it for so long. The hose was heavy, all the more so since it was still half-full of water.

Looking to the heavens for inspiration, I found it. Along the kitchen-alcove ceiling were three strings, apparently intended for drying laundry next to the hot-water pipes. I considered hanging the showerhead from one of them. If I hung it from the "far side" of the tiny alcove, with a little encouragement, I could probably coax out most of the remaining water. The only issue was whether the clothesline would support the weight of the hose.

My shoulder beginning to ache, with my free hand I positioned the stool under the strings. Doing my best to keep an eye not only on the unwieldy hose itself—which continued its serpentine flailing—but also the three strings, the ceiling, and the shelves, I climbed back onto the stool and hoisted the hose into the air. Despite my caution, I bumped into one of the shelves, sending a bottle of thyme crashing to the floor, where it shattered. Dreading the thought of how much thyme I had lost, I didn't look down. Instead, I stayed focused on the rebellious hose, the vertiginous change of perspective, and the small, wobbly stool on which I was now struggling to maintain a tenuous balance.

I hung the showerhead on a clothesline. The string didn't break.

I lowered myself back to the ground, careful to avoid the broken glass. I then began massaging the hose. Like a therapy patient reluctant to let go of the past, at first, the hose resisted. But then slowly, as though trusting my encouraging words and gentle touch, water began coming out. As I moved from one section of hose to the next, so much water abruptly broke into the bin that I almost feared a fully formed fetus might follow. Instead, several cumbersome minutes later, my body covered in sweat, with a final noisy splatter—less like a birth, more like a colonic—the hose emptied itself.

I may not have been the father of a newborn, but I was almost as happy as one.

After pausing to catch my breath and massage my shoulder, it was time to empty the bin. A relatively straightforward task, it entailed little more than a test of strength. As long as the bin wasn't too heavy and I didn't rush, it would be fine. I just had to make sure to avoid a spill, the "big mess" of which Stéphane had warned.

I grabbed two edges of the bin, one at the bottom and another on a side, making sure to bend from the knees. When I had been confined inside it moments earlier, the bin had seemed insufferably small. Now that I had to pick it up, it felt not only incomprehensibly large but dangerously unwieldy. The water inside surged from one end to the other. It threatened to spill over the edges and cascade onto the floor. It threw me off balance.

Before water flew from the bin, I managed to set it on the edge of the sink. Even that was risky: I wasn't sure how long the little sink could support the bin's weight. Not wanting to find out, I rushed to dump out all evidence of my first shower. Water gushed forth, swirling down the drain. The sink remained affixed to the wall.

As I savored yet another victory, I felt a trickle on my foot. I looked down. Several rivulets of water were streaming from beneath the shower curtains. They reminded me of school children who had wet themselves, but were too embarrassed to let anyone know.

Like an alarmed parent switching into crisis mode, I grabbed the first towel I could find, throwing it under the curtains, and wiping up the water before it got further out of hand. I then reached up to the sink for the bin, and placed it under the curtains. It hadn't occurred to me I'd need to wait for them to dry. I was new at this, I reminded myself; the lack of foresight was understandable.

Although it took four or five times longer than anticipated, ultimately, my first shower was a success. There had been some challenges, but no disasters. All the same, contemplating the curtains, looking at the bin, recalling the feel of plastic groping my skin, I decided my first was also my final; there would be no more showers. From there on out, I would be taking baths—or, at least as close as I could get, given what I had to work with.

I never thought my studio was paradise. I was captivated by the view of the Eiffel Tower, reminding me night after night that I was realizing my long-standing dream of living in Paris.

And I was excited and grateful for the chance to live alone in a very nice part of the city. The room was rough around the edges, but my survival instincts kept me from getting too close to them. I focused on the positives and overlooked the negatives.

One of the beautiful things about friends is that they help us see things about ourselves that we either can't or don't want to see. In this case, my friend Barb, who booked a last-minute spring-break trip to visit me in Paris, was about to call attention to things I either couldn't or didn't want to see about my sanctuary in the sky.

"Six years!" she exclaimed in disgust, upon learning how long Stéphane had lived in the room.

"I mean, it's no reflection on you," she reassured me, looking around at the tiny space. "I just can't believe that anyone could live here for six years!"

She was flabbergasted.

I wasn't sure how to react. I honestly hadn't thought it was that bad.

"It's cruddy," she snapped, when I tried to temper one of her insults. Without moving from her place on the futon, she then got specific.

I don't remember where she started. Maybe it was with the mass of electrical cords on the floor near the foot of the bed, like a pile of kindling threatening to go up in flames at any moment. Maybe it was the debate she had with herself about whether the stains on the walls or the ones on the carpet were more unsightly. It might have been her comments about the claustrophobic effect of the countless storage containers stacked not only from floor to ceiling in multiple places, but also on ceiling-level shelves around the perimeter of the apartment. It could have been her keen observation that the sleeping bag on the bed looked as though it had been around since someone's childhood ("That thing is disgusting!" she cried so emphatically I wondered if I should get her a bucket). Likewise, it could have been her comment that, though admirable in its functionality, the hanging table had been created with no concern whatsoever for aesthetics. "It's definitely a hardware-store table," she noted, with the disdain of someone mere months away from being awarded a Master of Fine Arts.

Then, of course, there were the impossible-to-defend oil and smoke stains on the wall above the butane stove, the paper holding together the broken windowpane, and the shelf that was so narrow it provided the constant threat (on which it had repeatedly delivered) of falling spices and broken glass.

Caught off guard, I'm not sure what came first, nor what followed—or in what order. All I know is that by the time her tirade had come to an end, no stain, shortcoming, or danger had been overlooked by Barb's critical eye.

"It's a shithole," she summarized, adding that the most striking aspect of the whole experience wasn't any of the apartment's innumerable faults, but "just the fact that somebody could live like this."

I had no reply. Though not without its undeniable quirks and unusual challenges, for two months the little room had worked just fine for me.

Given her disgust at the place I temporarily called home, it was ironic that Barb would make her own contribution to its decline. Still more ironic was her unconscious choice to do so the day before my departure. Given everything I had to do not only to see her off but to prepare to be on my own way, her timing could not have been worse.

It all began as I lay half-conscious on the futon, pleasantly aware of little more than the rich, fortifying smell of a dark roast of coffee percolating mere inches—for a reason that, to this day, escapes me—from my feet. Interrupting what, until then, had been seventh-floor-shithole serenity, I heard an "Oops!" followed by an even less welcome "Oh, gosh," which might as well have been a "This is more serious than I thought."

Still, given that it didn't seem life or death, with more curiosity than concern I asked, "What's wrong?"

"Oh, just spilled a little coffee," was Barb's reply.

"No big deal," I said, imagining a brown puddle on the kitchen tile. No doubt it would be cleaned up before I even got out of bed.

"Well, I don't know," Barb confessed, hesitating. "It's on the carpet."

"The carpet?" I asked, jolted awake—and hoping I had misunderstood.

"Yeah, I'm sorry," she said, scurrying around to address the situation while there was still any hope of addressing it.

Like a responsible backpacker, I had a policy of not only leaving no trace, but leaving the places I stayed in better shape than I found them. In this case, that shouldn't have been much of a challenge. But now Barb had made a big black spot in the middle of the baby-blue floor.

My mind jumped to possible repercussions. Would I be paying to have the nasty carpet professionally cleaned, finally, decades after it had been installed? Worse still, would this prove to be the excuse the owners needed to at long last replace it, kindly requesting I foot the bill?

Barb had already doused the affected area with an ineffectual combination of soap and water. Quickly deducing that a more specialized cleanser was required, I jumped onto the Internet, scouring it for something with which to scour the stain. Meanwhile, it was fast sinking deeper and deeper into each fiber of the sullied carpet.

The next half hour saw a desperate, haphazard assault of water, soap, lemon juice, vinegar, salt, and carpet cleaner thrown at the blemished area, leaving it saturated but not discernibly any cleaner. I decided to dry it out. Maybe that would show our efforts had not been entirely in vain.

First though, I had to say a quick goodbye to Barb. She had a plane to catch. She was leaving me to deal with her mess on my own.

Closing the door behind her, I grabbed a hairdryer from the

kitchen alcove. I plugged it in, turned it on, and got to work. To speed things up, I held the barrel of the dryer directly on the stain, hoping to get as much air as possible down to the base of the fibers. The dryer's tiny motor revved like a race-car engine at a starting line. Not wanting it to blow up in my hand, I made a point of lifting it off the carpet each time it seemed to approach its breaking point.

At least that's what I thought I was doing.

With a mysterious pop and a telltale smell, things took another turn for the worse. Having little experience with hairdryers, I had gone too far.

My initial thought was that the dryer had shorted out. Looking around, I realized that the overhead light was no longer on and the clock on the Internet router had gone black. I had blown a fuse. Better than the illegal butane tank, I consoled myself.

What now? Where was the fuse box? Was it even in the room? And what about the hairdryer? Was I going to have to buy a new one? My last hours in the little hovel were spiraling out of control. Every time I turned around, there was a new disaster with which to contend—and less time to deal with it.

Through a waft of smoke, on the opposite wall I spied a little metal door. I jumped to my feet, opened the door, and found myself face-to-face with the first good news I'd had since waking up to a caffeinated oil slick. I flipped the fuse that was out of synch with the rest. The light came back on and the router clock began blinking, calling out to be reset.

Maybe, I reasoned, eager for any excuse not to have to spend the time and money to buy a new one, the hairdryer wasn't really such a disaster either. Maybe it still had some life left in it. I held it at arm's length and—closing my eyes and preparing to jump for the futon—I flipped the switch.

Without a bang, on it came. There was no smoke, no menacing revving nor flesh-burning sparks. Immensely relieved, I decided no one needed to know about the hairdryer's near-death experience. I unplugged it, wrapped the cord around the handle, and returned the dryer to the shelf in the alcove—exactly as I had found it. No one would suspect I had ever laid a hand on it.

Turning my attention back to the stain, I could no longer ignore the sad truth: it didn't look any better. Actually, it looked worse—but not from being dried out. It was the scrubbing. It had left the stained fibers clumped and worn. If the black hole didn't call attention to the spill, the lumpy, nearly threadbare patches surely would.

It hadn't occurred to me that the carpet might wear away so quickly, practically disintegrating upon contact with soap and water, like one of those ancient Egyptian relics that turn to dust upon being exposed to air for the first time in millennia. I should have stopped scrubbing and acknowledged my defeat much earlier. What was I going to do now?

Only one thing came to mind.

I went downstairs and hurried to the closest supermarket. First making sure I wasn't overlooking any other possibilities, I headed to the art supplies section. When it was apparent nothing there met my needs, I went in search of help.

"Do you have any eye shadow in this color?" I asked a woman in cosmetics. I held up a piece of fuzz from an unsoiled section of the carpet.

A tall, strikingly attractive African-French woman, she took a moment before responding, looking me up and down. Deciding it was better to explain the situation than to let her imagine it for herself, I described the coffee incident. My last-ditch hope was that the right shade of eye shadow might help conceal the damage, like foundation covering up a hickey.

Relieved to have an ally in my struggle, I walked with the woman from brand to brand of cosmetics. Exploring each color palette, we held the piece of fuzz next to every shade of blue that might be a match. When we found one on which we both agreed, I told the woman I'd take it.

"You know," she taunted with a wry smile, "you can do more with that than cover coffee stains."

I laughed, thanked her again for her help, and was on my way.

My sense of urgency distracting me from the seven-flight climb, with the ease of a helium balloon taking to the air, I flew up the stairs and headed for the room. Closing the door behind me, I fell to my knees, opened the shopping bag, and took out the eye shadow. Was it the right color? Would it take hold?

Those and other questions looming like the end of a cliffhanger, I took the eye-shadow applicator in hand and, as though inspired to create something of beauty, dabbed it against a virgin patch of carpet.

I gasped.

It was a match.

But would it cover the coffee stain?

I put more eye shadow on the brush, and began applying it to the soiled fibers. It was clear that, if my approach were going to work, it was going to require a tremendous amount of eye shadow. Losing myself in my unlikely canvas, I applied more blue. And more still.

It wasn't long before I grew frustrated. And increasingly anxious. I wasn't seeing the results I wanted—the results I needed. Rather than cover up the coffee, I appeared to merely be diluting it. Instead of applying eye shadow, it was as if I were adding cream, molasses black turning a bluish gray. The new color was better than prior to the makeover; but it wasn't good enough.

I threw the eye-shadow brush to the floor.

I had failed.

I hoped the big black stain wouldn't come back to haunt me a month later, when Stéphane and María returned from their travels.

When I moved out of the apartment, having found a much nicer one in an even better location (and with a full-size bathtub, though the toilet was still at the end of the hall), I had no idea I'd again be face-to-face with the coffee stain in less than a week's time.

Although they hadn't asked for a deposit, it did occur to Stéphane and María not to let me slip away without a walk-through. Their friend Caroline would do the honors. I would also give her the keys.

Perhaps it was just my imagination. Or paranoia. But, from the start, Caroline seemed suspicious; specifically, she seemed suspicious of me. Whereas my emails to her were warm and friendly, her replies were cold and distant. I began to dread how she would react to the black hole in the carpet, the source of ongoing nightmares since my departure.

When the day of reckoning came, I found myself back on the old metro line, getting off at the old stop. Strange to think it had been mine for two months.

As I approached the apartment building, Caroline was nowhere to be found. I assumed she had yet to arrive. Upon closer inspection, I discovered a note with my name on it wedged into the door. My heart skipped a beat. Rather than wait for me downstairs as agreed, Caroline had snuck into the apartment on her own. I felt deceived—and outsmarted. There was no longer any doubt: I was about to answer for my crimes.

I ascended the staircase and knocked on the door to the room.

"*Entrez,*" came a voice from inside.

I expected a scene of the sort usually reserved for murder investigations, white chalk outlining the coffee stain, the sullied patch of carpet cordoned off with police tape to prevent nosy onlookers from getting too close—all of it supervised by a tough woman known for being one hell of an investigator.

I opened the door. The room was exactly as I had left it. The only exception was an attractive woman in her late-twenties, who welcomed me with a warm smile.

"*Salut,*" she said, extending her hand, "*Je suis Caroline.*"

"*Salut,*" I replied, finding her pleasant demeanor suspect.

"Well, the place looks great!" she declared, taking one more look in the kitchen.

"It does?"

I was perspiring profusely, both from the climb and my

nerves.

"Yeah, it does," she replied, turning her attention back to me with another smile—one I trusted even less than the first.

"Um, okay. Good."

Dumbfounded, I wasn't particularly verbose. Didn't she see it? It was big. It was black. Realizing I was staring at it, I wrested my attention away and back to her pretty gaze.

An awkward pause followed. Nothing occurred to me to say.

"Do you have the keys?"

"Oh yeah! The keys!" I reached into my pocket and practically threw them at her.

"Well, I guess that's it then," she said, taking one last look around—still somehow oblivious to the horrendous stain. It was like standing at the window without seeing the Eiffel Tower. How could she possibly overlook it? Did she have a stiff neck? Some sort of tunnel vision that prevented her from seeing the floor?

Whatever the reason, I could ponder it later. I had just been given the all clear. There was no point in pressing my luck by extending my visit a moment longer.

Caroline and I accompanied each other downstairs, chitchatting like old pals. Even once outside, we continued talking for a while.

"Well, maybe I'll see you when Stéphane and María get back," she offered.

"Yeah, hope so!" I said with an overenthusiastic smile. The end of the ordeal combined with the adrenaline rush for the duration had suddenly made me giddy. I needed to leave before I said or did something stupid.

And leave I did, never to look back.

A month later Stéphane and María sent me an effusive email thanking me for taking such great care of their place.

There was no mention of the stain.

3 NO STOPPING

I was in my mid-twenties, backpacking in Eastern Europe. I believe I was in Romania. It might have been Hungary. Come to think of it, maybe it wasn't even Eastern Europe at all. Maybe I was on Guam. What I do know is that I had just arrived at a youth hostel. It was located in a converted old school, a multi-story edifice with the predictable warmth and charm of architecture designed by left-brained civic bureaucrats.

I checked in, dropped my things in my room, and went back downstairs. Other young travelers relaxed in a maze of sofas, the lobby alive with language and laughter. Here and there, backpacks got in the way, like obstacles on a course. City maps and tourist brochures littered tables. Soda cans fizzed and snack food wrappers rustled. Guidebooks offered indispensable advice.

I was chatting with a Swedish guy and a Danish girl, when I realized I needed to go to the bathroom. Caught up in the conversation, I had been paying more attention to it than to my body. I had waited too long—and now I couldn't wait any longer. I really had to go.

The young attendant at the front desk looked up from his computer just long enough to gesture to a door on the other side of the room. From where I was standing, it appeared to open onto little more than darkness.

"That way," he said, returning to his work.

Through the door I discovered a long corridor. As I proceeded down it, it felt as though I'd crossed over to a different building. This one felt forgotten, left behind in some obscure past. Stale air smelled of wood rot, mildew, and dust— of time itself, perhaps. Many years had elapsed since not only children but fresh breezes had run up and down these halls. A couple of bulbs overhead were burnt out, as though they'd given up hope, while those still clinging to life shed little light, the mood all the more oppressive for it. And then there was the floor; no one had swept it in ages. It felt gritty beneath my feet.

Continuing down the hall, I peered into abandoned classrooms. I saw dusty tables and chairs in disarray, debris gathered beneath them. Blinds on sunless windows climbed up or hung down, as if unable to make up their minds. Some had one end stuck higher than the other, spreading them open like silk fans. I half expected to see the ghosts of tortured teachers or possessed children, forever trapped in a haunted past. Ostensibly, though, I was alone.

I rounded a corner. Delving further into the silence, I felt that much more removed from my new friends in the common area—like being in the ocean and losing sight of the shore. *You won't be here for long*, I reminded myself. I had to pee so badly, I'd finish almost as soon as I started.

An opening without a door revealed a restroom, its interior gray like stone, its floor concrete. A row of urinals lined one wall, their porcelain discolored and marred with indecipherable stains. Some stalls were located on the opposite side of the room, which was so surprisingly large I wondered if it had originally been used for some other purpose. There was a bench in the middle. It was even darker here than in the hall.

Eager to get my business over and done with, I unzipped my pants. A powerful stream gushed forth. A bottle of champagne uncorked, I steadied myself on the wall, afraid of being thrown backward. I was delirious with relief. Why does it feel so much better to pee when we hold it so much longer than we should, when our bladders are about to burst? Why is there such a perverse correlation between the pleasure and the pain preceding it? It doesn't make sense. Neither does it matter. Not really. I continued relishing the release.

Until I heard something unusual.

My eyes rolled back into my head, at first I ignored my ears. But it was too loud. And persistent.

The sound of water.

It was splattering, as though something somewhere in the bathroom had sprung a leak—something close at hand. I looked around, my piss still streaming full throttle. I hoped the force of it didn't crack the aged porcelain.

Then, before I could pinpoint the noise, I felt something on my shoes.

As my eyes went toward the floor, through the hole in the urinal I saw something else; something that had been there all along, but that I had overlooked in the relative darkness.

My feet.

There was no pipe attached to the urinal.

I was peeing on the floor.

I panicked. Reflexively, with all my might, I tried to slam on the brakes. I made a desperate attempt to squeeze my prostate—or whatever muscle or organ it was down there controlling the flow. It was too late. The floodgates had not merely opened; given the sheer magnitude of the deluge, they'd been disabled. They'd be useless until the entire reservoir had been drained.

No longer master of my own body, I watched in horror as I continued to pee on the bathroom floor. I moved my feet back slightly, but there was little else I could do. Out of a misplaced sense of propriety—and, no doubt, habit—I kept directing the flow into the urinal. As if it mattered. As if it somehow made it less offensive than taking another step back and just peeing directly into my ever-expanding pool. There was no drain in the floor. The pee had nowhere to go. It was as powerless as I was.

Meanwhile, I glanced at the urinals on either side of mine. They didn't have pipes connected to them either. None of the urinals did. Why wasn't there a sign or maybe even a rope to prevent people from using them? Who bothered to make sure their urinal was hooked up to the plumbing before they took a piss?

As I pondered those questions and more, my marathon stream finally ran its course. Catching my breath, I zipped my pants and stepped away from the urinal. The large puddle reflected a lone light bulb—a full moon glimmering on the smooth surface of a pitch-black pond.

I looked around for a mop or towels or something to clean up the mess. There wasn't anything—not even soap next to the sinks. Was I even in the right bathroom? I had to be. The guy at the front desk had simply pointed to the door—he hadn't given me any other instructions.

Consequently, now I was going to have to give him some very bad news.

I glanced one last time at the shiny puddle of pee—still in disbelief—before turning to begin the long, dark walk down the corridor back to the lobby.

Why did it feel like a walk of shame? I hadn't done anything wrong. It wasn't my fault. Right?

All the same, as I took one heavy step after another, my shoe squeaking from having stepped in pee, this time I didn't glance into the dusty classrooms or pay any mind to the grit under my feet or notice the stale smell on the air. I was too preoccupied, faced as I was with a daunting moral dilemma.

I knew I should tell the front-desk attendant what I had done. It was the right thing to do. Even though it wasn't my fault. Otherwise, how would the hostel know to clean up the mess?

But, again, it wasn't my fault. It was ridiculous that they had a wall of urinals that no one had bothered to connect to the plumbing. It was like some sort of gag staged for a hidden-camera show. Why should I have to fess up to a crime for which I'd been set up, one I had committed only on account of someone else's ineptitude?

I didn't want to. I didn't want to tell an indignant teenager that I had peed on his floor—and that now he was going to have to clean it up. I didn't want to have to walk down the creepy hall a third time, the hostel worker escorting me like a police officer to the scene of a crime—my crime. I didn't want to stand with him next to the murky black pool confessing that, yes, officer, the urine you see before you is in fact my urine. I did that. I peed on the floor of a building, inside, like a puppy who's not yet potty trained or a senile old cat who's not only lost most of its fur but control of its bladder, too.

That would not have been right either. And—it now occurred to me—I didn't actually have to do it: I didn't have to tell the attendant what had happened. While the ghosts of forgotten teachers or the spirits of former students might have borne witness to my little accident, not a single other living soul knew about it.

I got it. It suddenly made sense. I suddenly understood why my stroll back to the lobby felt like a walk of shame. It wasn't because of what I *had* done. It was because of what I was *not* going to do.

And, in spite of how bad I felt for whomever was destined to find what I had left behind, in spite of my shame for setting someone else up much like I myself had just been set up, I didn't.

4 BARELY BREATHING

My bladder was about to burst.

I had just arrived at my friend Sophie's Paris apartment, where I had stayed a few times before. The trip from Charles de Gaulle had been a long one. I worked my way through multiple airport terminals, weaving through crowds from every nation speaking just as many languages, past boisterous families and stone-faced business travelers and eager backpackers. I spent over an hour on the train, pausing at one gray suburban stop after another, scarcely any indication we were approaching the City of Lights. I navigated three different subway lines, seeing myself reflected in the eyes of a rat as I scurried through one subterranean tunnel after another. Finally, I emerged from Sophie's stop and walked to her building, several blocks away. The air smelled of urban grime, of dust and exhaust, of odors I made a conscious effort to ignore. It was infernally hot.

As soon as I set foot in the apartment, I dropped my backpack and did a quick 180, turning to what the uninitiated might assume was a small closet door. I knew better. As in so many Victorians at home in San Francisco, the toilet had been sentenced to solitary confinement, no doubt for a crime it hadn't even committed. I opened the door and closed it behind me.

It was a peculiar sort of homecoming. A roll of the industrial-strength pink toilet paper Sophie always bought—thick enough, I suspected, to use in a printer—lay on the carpeted floor. There was no place to hang it. A calendar from last year was still posted on the back of the door. Now, like then, I was struck by the impressive number of canonized martyrs, each day set aside for one, if not multiple, saints. A naked bulb dangled overhead from a frayed cord, a luminous corpse hanging from a poorly executed noose.

As I got down to business, it felt like being back on the plane. The walls were mere inches away, as was the door. Despite being of average height, I had almost no leg room. I was closed in on all sides.

It didn't help that there were no windows, an unforgivable design flaw repeated over and over in contemporary buildings. When will architects concede that those pathetic, rattly little fans aren't even remotely as effective as the simple act of opening a window to let in some fresh air? Never mind their failure to let in even a single ray of sunlight. No matter. In this case, the question was moot: the bathroom didn't have a fan. There was no ventilation whatsoever. The temperature rose, and I became more and more uncomfortable.

I tried to move things along, but my body was not *d'accord*. It was too out of whack from traveling halfway around the world. Attempting to force the issue only made things worse. The air got stuffier. My breath shortened. I became lightheaded. What little fluids were left in my body poured out of my skin, evaporating into the thickening air. When the walls began to glisten, I knew I was entering dangerous territory. I had to ease up, lest Sophie come home to a tragic reenactment of Elvis's final moments.

I threw open the door.

Why had I closed it? Sophie wasn't even there.

I had hoped for a refreshing burst of cool air. I was disappointed. Nothing happened. I heard sounds from the street several stories below, but the living-room curtains didn't move. They might as well have been made of stone.

Eventually the ordeal was over. When it was, I did what I should have done the moment I arrived: article by article, I shed every piece of clothing. They had practically melded to my skin. If I waited any longer, I'd be chafed from head to toe. My shirt and jeans, my underwear and socks. I let them all fall to the ground as though, rather than saturated with sweat, they were consumed by flames.

I looked down at the steaming pile of clothes.

I headed for the shower.

The bathroom was larger than the water closet. However, since the apartment had no closets, the bathroom did double duty. Not only was it full of boxes, it also served as a storage room for random piles of tubes and messy tangles of wires. It looked as though Sophie had looted a hardware store and stolen a bunch of junk she'd never use. Was this what the early stages of hoarding looked like? Whatever the case, like its banished counterpart next door, the bathroom was incredibly confining.

All the more so when I got into the tub.

Or, rather, when I climbed up to the tub.

Perched on a platform whose *raison d'être* I struggled to guess, the bathtub was raised a couple of feet off the floor. It was a peculiar setup, one I'd never seen before and haven't come across since.

My first attempt at taking a shower was a struggle. The bathtub's unusual elevation was not offset by higher than usual ceilings. Again my being of only average height proved advantageous, since my head nearly touched the ceiling. But I wasn't just restricted overhead; the situation behind me was just as problematic. Clotheslines over the back of the tub made the space even more cramped, a web in which one wrong slip was sure to leave me entangled in hosiery, panties, and bras. The world was once again closing in on me.

Only by paying meticulous attention did I manage to

shower without incident. When I was done, I turned off the water. Through a lingering cloud of steam, I then looked at the floor, the lines in the tile like an urban grid viewed from 30,000 feet in the sky. It felt so far away.

Taking my time, I executed the precarious descent back down to Earth, being careful not to slip on any of the wet surfaces. As I did, I couldn't help but wonder, was I missing something? Amidst all the clutter, was I overlooking a step stool? A rope ladder? An inflatable slide? Sophie was very short. If it was a struggle for me to climb in and out of the shower, it must have been even harder for her.

The temperature and humidity didn't make my descent any easier, both having soared while I bathed. Like the water closet, the bathroom lacked a window. What's more, when I paused to catch my breath, I observed a tiny, dust-covered duct next to the showerhead. The heat and moisture—never mind the dark mildew flourishing on the walls and ceiling—suddenly made much more sense.

Showering, on the other hand, no longer made any sense at all.

The bathroom now indistinguishable from a sauna, by the time I made it back down to the floor, my body was dripping with sweat. It was as if the shower for which I'd risked life and limb had never even happened.

More miserable with each passing moment, I wrapped myself in a towel and went to open the door. My hand on the knob, I stopped myself.

The door.

Why had I closed it? Why hadn't I learned my lesson the first time around, in the water closet? Sophie still wasn't home, after all.

Chastising myself for yet another oversight, I flung the door open and headed straight for the living room.

It was stuffy in here, too; but it wasn't nearly as bad as what I had just left behind. I didn't sit down. My body was wet, and drying it off wasn't much use, since I was still sweating profusely. Instead, I approached the window. Pedestrians made their ways along sidewalks. A few cars drove down the narrow, one-way street. An old woman dumped her recyclables into a dumpster, glass bottles making their cumbersome, short-lived music as they tumbled through the air, shattering in a dramatic crescendo.

When I'd waited long enough, I went back to the bathroom. Leaving the door open behind me, like a rock climber scaling the same route twice in one day, again I made my way up to the bathtub.

Whereas before I'd nearly passed out in the stifling steam, now I could hardly have felt more alive.

An ice-cold shower never felt so good.

5 FRESHLY SQUEEGED

I may as well have come from the other side of the world.

The flight from Paris to Copenhagen takes little more than an hour, but the flight was only one part of my journey. The trip to Charles de Gaulle seemed endless: the long walk to the metro; three different subway lines; an hour-long train ride; the chaos as I made my way to my terminal; and, once there, the unpleasant interaction with a smug Dane who brazenly cut in front of me—and wasn't happy when I called him out in front of his two blond-haired, blue-eyed children. Then, in the pre-boarding area, the passengers were informed our flight had been delayed. When we finally boarded, it turned out we'd missed our departure window. We wouldn't be going anywhere for at least another hour.

By the time I arrived in Copenhagen, I was exhausted. And I felt as greasy as a fried fish.

My friend, Aksel, met me in the airport. He lived in a charming old building in the center of town. As soon as we walked up the stairs to his apartment and stepped inside, he handed me a towel and ushered me to the bathroom. I'm not sure who wanted me to shower more—me or him.

I flipped on the bathroom light, closing the door behind me. I was surprised by how small the room was. It was more like a walk-in closet than a full-fledged room.

I looked around. To my immediate left, a tiny sink. On the other side of it, a toilet. Along the wall to my right, a few shallow, sparse shelves.

Something was missing. Something essential.

Where was the shower?

I looked around again, quickly reminded: there wasn't anyplace else to look.

Had I taken a wrong turn? Maybe the toilet was in one room and the shower in another? But there hadn't been any doors in the hallway other than those to the kitchen and bedroom. Besides, my friend had personally escorted me to the room in which I was now standing.

I was where I was supposed to be.

Would the shower be joining me?

Maybe it, too, had troubles at the airport? A delayed flight? A disagreement with a rude Dane that escalated into a full-on brawl, as opposed to my mere little tiff?

I looked around yet again, a little more closely. A few toiletries sat on the shelves. A navy blue towel hung on the back of the door. I again scanned the room, convinced I was missing something glaringly obvious.

I was.

Literally under my nose.

We see what we want to see. We overlook what we don't expect.

What I hadn't expected was the showerhead to be lying on the back of the airplane-bathroom-size sink. Yet there it was, oblivious to my conundrum. Or, perhaps instead, it was resting quietly like some woodland creature hoping to go unnoticed, deliberately frozen in place and refraining from making even the slightest sound that might alert me to its presence.

Like most European showerheads, this one was connected to a flexible metal hose. The hose was connected to the faucet over the sink.

Having found the showerhead, I was halfway there.

But where was I supposed to use it?

Inspecting my surroundings, I searched for a sign—on the walls, the shelves, the back of the door. It wasn't until I glanced at my feet that I stumbled upon two clues: a drain in the middle of the floor and a squeegee under the sink.

Aha!

The possibility hadn't even occurred to me. Now I got it.

I was already in the shower.

I laughed, happy to have solved the mystery and eager to get down to business.

There were only a few inches between the toilet and the walls boxing it in, leaving no place to bathe. The only option, then, was the confined area behind the door, between the sink and the shelves. In other words, where I was already standing.

There was a shower curtain that could be—although it wasn't clear if it was supposed to be (when I asked him later, my friend didn't know either)—pulled closed to divide the room in half. Ordinarily that might have been a great idea. Given the circumstances, I failed to see how further limiting my movement could possibly be advantageous. I tried closing the curtain, only to confirm my suspicions: I couldn't move, not without coming into repeated contact with the dingy fabric. The curtain had clearly been in the apartment longer than my friend—and it hadn't aged nearly as well. I stuffed it back into the tight space between the wall and the shelves, the mildew spreading upward from its edges no doubt relieved to return to the darkness.

I turned on the water and, at long last, made my first attempt to shower. It met with mixed success.

Try and try as I might, I still could not figure out where to stand, and I had no idea what to do with the showerhead. I couldn't put it back on the sink while the water was running—the water would have gotten everywhere. But I couldn't turn the faucet off, either. Achieving the right water temperature had proved such a tricky balancing act, I was reluctant to have to start over.

Holding the showerhead was no less problematic, since producing a soapy lather is impossible with just one hand.

Seeing no other option, I resigned myself to letting the water run, while I pinned the showerhead under my foot. What I hadn't anticipated was how much the showerhead would writhe around on the floor. Like an incensed serpent, it flailed about, dousing everything in the room with its errant spray.

So much for worrying about getting water everywhere.

Watching water drip from the sides of the toilet, it occurred to me that my friend never had to go to the trouble of washing it. It also occurred to me that, were I so-inclined, I could simultaneously shower and use the toilet. I was hard-pressed, however, to imagine under what circumstances I might find myself so-inclined.

Fatigue from my travels setting in, I finished my first shower in Copenhagen. It hadn't been easy, but I had pulled it off. A little perseverance goes a long way.

After cracking the bathroom door to let out some steam, I dried myself off and squeegeed the floor, pushing the water down the drain. I then directed my attention to my teeth.

Putting toothpaste on my toothbrush, I turned the water on again. As I leaned toward the sink, I had to stop mid-stoop. I wasn't sure if the sink was too small or the faucet too long, but what was certain was that they were horribly mismatched. The faucet extended so far from its base that it almost touched the edge of the basin. Moistening my toothbrush without leaving globs of toothpaste on the faucet or sink required a surgeon's calm precision. Washing my hands would be nearly impossible.

Weren't the Danes known for design?

I recalled that the Copenhagen store in San Francisco had met its demise many years earlier.

Returning my attention to the task at hand, I managed to get enough water onto my toothbrush to brush my teeth. Once I was done, I nonchalantly spit out a day's worth of bacterial buildup, just as I had countless times before.

I flinched. Out of nowhere, I felt like a bird had shat on my feet.

I looked down. The sink was so small, I had missed the mark. Less than half of the toothpaste lather had fallen into the tiny porcelain bowl, the rest either landing on my bare feet or splattering all over the freshly-squeegeed floor.

Damn it.

I rushed to wipe off the minty-fresh droppings before they whitened my skin, and gave the floor another squeege. Then I got out my dental floss.

My pre-departure visit to the dentist had been a bloody mess, full of dire warnings about the debilitating consequences of a mouth blighted by gingivitis. The fact that I had no cavities meant nothing. On the contrary, I was told my saliva had an exceptionally high mineral content, which meant I had to be even more vigilant than most about dental hygiene (and schedule another visit in six months, as opposed to my normal twelve; and, buy an electric toothbrush, which they had on sale in the office—no pressure). A little unseen spool spun briefly, and I snapped off a strand.

I didn't have much history working with dental floss. As a result, a mirror was indispensable for navigating the cavernous world enveloping my yellowed teeth and bleeding gums. Having wrapped one end of the floss around my right index finger and the other around my left, I looked up, expecting to find a stunningly handsome face reflected back at me.

Instead I found a polished piece of metal.

It hung inches from my face, deceptively positioned where a mirror should have been, as though doing its best to fill the role. And, in all fairness, in the stainless-steel medicine cabinet door, I was, in fact, able to discern a vague, distorted version of myself trapped in some distant, out-of-reach reality. Distracted by my beguiling search for the shower, I had failed to notice that the bathroom also lacked a mirror.

How did the Danes all look so good? On the other hand, perhaps sparing themselves the daily horror of puffy faces, baggy eyes, and unsightly blemishes burst to the surface overnight accounted—at least in part—for why they were the happiest people in the world. Maybe we all needed to get rid of our mirrors.

Whatever the case, I had just been given a perfect excuse

not to floss.

I wadded up the unsullied string, ready to be rid of it in a single, self-satisfied toss. But, looking around, I could not find a trash can. There wasn't one of those either. I'd have to take the dental floss with me and throw it away in the kitchen.

When, at long last, I prepared to leave the bathroom behind, I realized there was one more thing I needed to do: I needed to pee.

Stepping over to the toilet, I raised the lid.

With a loud splash, a small tsunami cascaded to the floor, soaking my feet.

A pool of water had collected on the toilet seat during my shower. Since it was transparent, I hadn't noticed it—until it was all over me and the floor.

I got the squeegee back out, and wiped down the bathroom floor a third time.

I wish I could say I learned my lesson, that, like putting a hand onto a hot burner, I didn't need to learn it a second time. Sadly, that would not be an honest retelling of the facts. The first tsunami proved to be just one of many, each leaving me more frustrated than the last. For whatever reason, I could not get it into my head to check for water on the toilet seat after every shower.

I'd also like to be able to say that I quickly adapted to the peculiarities of the bathroom in Copenhagen. Apart from my discovery of an overlooked place to rest the showerhead (one that had eluded my friend, I might add), I can't say I ever really did.

If those peculiarities had left me in any way unappreciative, that all changed when I learned that, even today, individual apartments in many of Copenhagen's historic buildings don't have showers at all. Bathing facilities are often still communal—even in updated residences with every other modern amenity.

Imagine my surprise when I discovered that the minuscule, idiosyncratic bathroom with which I'd been making do all week also turned out to be a relatively uncommon luxury.

6 DOUBLE DUTY

Malta had been on my radar for years, ever since reading about its uncommon density of UNESCO world heritage sites. The capital city alone, Valletta, was apparently full of them. It looked like a beautiful destination. All of Malta did, the pictures I saw calling to mind much of what I loved about the Mediterranean. The warm, singular glow of limestone was everywhere: in the old buildings, the massive walls holding back the sea, and the rugged cliffs plummeting into it. History was visible everywhere, too. The Templars had built a cathedral. Ancient civilizations had left behind an underground Neolithic necropolis and Megalithic stone temples. Then, of course, there was the Mediterranean itself, its glittering blue waters ever present.

I wanted to go to Malta.

So, when I was able to take three weeks off from work, I went.

Having spent a lot of time both living and traveling in the Mediterranean, I wasn't surprised to discover that much about Malta felt familiar. What I hadn't expected was for so much of that familiarity to stem from similarities to my own city, San Francisco. Valletta's streets rolled up and down steep hills. The buildings lining them peered out from bay windows. And, again, the sea was omnipresent, just like at home.

I rented a top-floor apartment in an old building in the center of Valletta. The owner, Milo, was a handsome and friendly, albeit anxious man in his thirties. Slight of frame though full of energy, he had smooth skin, full lips, and dark, wavy hair that was meticulously styled. Having comparatively little hair myself, I couldn't help but be a little jealous. I also couldn't help but wonder how much time went into the daily sculpting of his immaculately coiffed locks.

Milo lived across the hall. When he learned I was a writer, he remarked how lucky I was to lead the life I did. I wasn't given the chance to tell him I had yet to publish a single word and had no way of knowing if I ever would. That wasn't the point. The point was that Milo needed to express—to share with someone—his dissatisfaction with his own life. Who better for sharing intimacies with than a stranger?

Milo showed me the apartment. It was simple but stylish—though I did have to stop my eyes from rolling when I saw that one of the living-room walls served as the kitchen. The open-floor-plan concept had made it to Malta; I was old school, and still preferred partitions between my rooms. Reminding myself that the lamentable fad would run its course soon enough, I looked around the rest of the room. I admired the sofa, armchair, and coffee table, all of them colorful, sleek, and modern, with a distinctive retro flair. Almodóvar would have felt right at home. Don Draper would have been perfectly in his element.

I walked through a door next to the sink and found myself in the bedroom. It was about the same size as the living-dining-room-kitchen. Directly in front of me, I saw a full-size bed. To my right were two closet-like spaces, in reality just shelves covered with white muslin curtains. They did a poor job of concealing the closets' contents, which, at the moment, were limited to some plastic hangers and a bag of votive candles.

On the side of the room facing the street, I discovered an enclosed balcony. Its bottom half was comprised of wood panels. Above each was a window with its own shudder, most of which were open. I approached the enclosure and looked outside. I had great views of the city skyline, including a large church just down the street, as well as the narrow street itself, far below. I could also see shipping cranes in the port taking to the sky.

I immediately loved the little room. From another era, it had character. It was the kind of place I could easily spend hours writing away, happy and inspired, in my own world—and protected from the outside one, its distractions and annoyances. The room reminded me of the old Arab *mashrabiyas*, protruding windows enclosed with carved wood latticework, allegedly to allow women to observe the goings-on in the street without themselves being observed. Malta having inherited much from Arab culture, I suspected the balcony was a direct descendant of such enclosures.

The door to the bathroom was between the closets. I stepped inside, surprised by what I discovered. The bathroom was huge, perhaps half the size of the bedroom. The bathtub was huge, too, big enough for at least two, if not three people. Enough jets to go around, it was almost more akin to a hot tub.

The room had a tall window with a translucent pane. Looking outside, at ground level I saw a small grassy courtyard. Directly opposite, I saw another window.

Milo handed me the keys and headed across the hall. I poked around the apartment. A bottle of wine in the refrigerator. Thoughtful. Coffee, too, for the morning. I never made coffee at home—buying it was my ticket to the time I spent working in cafés—but I appreciated that gesture, as well.

I browsed through some tourist pamphlets on a desk next to the front door, unable to pay them much mind, given my fatigue. Instead, I stumbled to the bedroom. Moments later, clothes still on, I was facedown on the bed.

Until 5:00 AM.

That's when I woke up. It wasn't because of jet lag. I didn't wake up because my body was confused about where it was or what time it might be. I woke up because of something happening outside, in the little street four stories below.

At first I doubted what I heard. Jolted awake, I assumed I'd made a mistake, that I'd been dreaming. But then I heard it again. And again. Metal dragging and dropping and clanging against metal. Pounding followed, along with that hollow, almost musical reverberation aluminum makes when hammered.

Was there a construction site being set up outside my window?

Unlikely. Not at 5:00 AM.

I didn't move. I felt as though I hadn't slept a wink, and I had neither the strength nor the will to get up and go to the window. Whatever was happening, it couldn't go on forever. It was bound to stop. If I ignored it, hopefully I would just fall back asleep.

The pounding continued.

Ignoring it wasn't going to do the trick. I reached for the nightstand, and grabbed my earplugs, always standing by, at the ready.

After a few more minutes, the pounding still showed no signs of letting up. I was now even more convinced: it had to be some sort of construction. I couldn't fathom what else might account for the sorts of sounds I was hearing.

I covered my head with the pillow.

It didn't help.

It occurred to me that never in my life had covering my head with a pillow made any difference. Was I the only one for whom the timeless trick was utterly ineffective? Were there actually people out there who had successfully used a pillow to block out troublesome sound, the soft, fluffy barrier enough for them to slide back into an undisturbed slumber?

If so, I sure as hell wasn't one of them.

After another minute or two of denial, of delusional hope, I faced the sorry truth: the ruckus was not going to stop anytime soon.

I threw off the useless pillow, took out my earplugs, and let out a deep sigh. I stared up at the ceiling, barely able to make out anything in the darkness.

Occasional shouts now mixed with the generalized commotion. Someone was giving direction. Someone with a really big mouth and lungs the size of a whale. I wondered if he was an opera singer. If he couldn't sing, he should be in the theater. The man could project! His was a voice that belonged on stage.

A seagull let out a harsh cry, as though telling the Maltese Pavarotti to keep it down. I wasn't the only one who was annoyed.

I'd begun wiggling my toes at the far end of the bed, without realizing it. Even before I had, my body had foreseen how the situation was going to play out. It was rousing itself back to life. I now joined in, moving my toes deliberately, faster. A couple of more sighs gave way to a long, head-to-toe stretch, my back arching like a cat's. I was tempted to let out a frustrated shriek and maybe even a hiss, but didn't have the energy.

More metal crashed to the ground, the loudest noise yet. Had someone just knocked over thirty gongs?

With no small effort, I got up and walked toward the window. The floor teetered like a ship at sea, as I struggled to regain control of my body, my arms reflexively outstretched to help me balance. I felt like a fledgling who can't yet fly.

Opening a shutter, I looked down. Light blinded my eyes. When I glimpsed the street far below, I had to steady myself from a flash of vertigo.

I regrouped. I looked down again. This time, my eyes focused.

A flea market.

Metal rod after metal rod, up and down the street for blocks in both directions, vendors were erecting stalls. Once the rest of the city awoke (assuming there was anyone still asleep), swarms of bargain hunters in search of cheap clothing, handmade leather goods, and high-fashion knockoffs would overtake the narrow lane.

That was all fine and good. Who doesn't love cheap, shoddy, imported trinkets? But couldn't the vendors wait until a little later to set up? Would, say, 7:00 AM be unreasonable? Couldn't we at least talk about it?

I scanned the building across the street. No one was at any of the windows. Other than the seagull, was I the only one upset by the ruckus? Perhaps the neighbors had all been subjected to the insufferable racket so many times, they'd developed some sort of auditory immunity? Or, maybe they planned ahead. Maybe each night before the market, they got so shitfaced not a single one of them woke up before noon the next day—construction projects and washed-up opera stars be damned.

Whatever the case, somehow they were able to sleep though the hubbub.

I was not.

Unfortunate, given that being awake was so painful. Even under normal circumstances, 5:00 AM is no time to start the day. But I had just flown halfway around the world. I was already doomed to a brutal struggle with jet lag, the best way of dealing with it being to get onto the local schedule as quickly as possible. That was not going to happen if I couldn't get back to sleep.

As though afraid someone below might look up and see my tears of frustration, I closed the shutter and turned away from the window.

It was then that I saw it. Beyond the bed, a faint glow coming from the bathroom.

Like someone living a near-death experience, I began walking toward the light. It wasn't that I suddenly needed to pee. I hadn't forgotten to brush my teeth earlier. Something else was drawing me toward the bathroom. Something was waiting for me there.

I turned on the light.

There it was. I recognized it right away. The solution to my dilemma, the answer revealed in the emptiness.

I went back to the bedroom, flipping on the light there, too. I then walked over to the bed, put my hands under the mattress, and lifted it onto its side. It flopped one direction, then the other, like a giant slice of bread. It wasn't meant for standing upright. Like so many inept, cowardly politicians, it was spineless. Nevertheless, once it was more or less stable, I was able to slide it across the floor and into the bathroom. A burst of air flew up as I let it fall onto the ceramic tile.

I positioned the mattress the best I could. It abutted the wall, the bathtub, and the toilet. But it lay almost perfectly flat.

I paused to consider my handiwork. The living room had a refrigerator, oven, and sink. Somehow it seemed fitting that the bathroom have a bed. Maybe I'd put a washer and dryer in the bedroom and a treadmill in the *mashrabiya*.

I closed the bathroom door, put my earplugs back in, and turned off the light.

Flea market? What flea market?

Mere moments after closing my eyes, I'd already fallen back into a deep, peaceful slumber. I hoped the seagull had somehow found the same sort of solace.

An hour or two later I woke up to pee. Instinctively getting up to go to the bathroom, it hit me: I was already there. I laughed. Grateful for the uncustomary luxury of doing so without the inconvenience of leaving my bed, I crawled to the end of it, stood up, and relieved myself in the darkness.

7 BETWEEN MY LEGS

Ever since my first visit many years before, Barcelona had held a special place in my imagination. When friends I was visiting in Valencia mentioned they knew someone with an available room, I decided to head north for a month.

The apartment was in a nondescript old building in the Barceloneta. Traditionally a working-class neighborhood of fishermen and their families, today it is better known as home to some of the city's prime beaches. It is also a short stroll from many of its most interesting neighborhoods and attractions. El Raval, the Gothic Quarter, and las Ramblas are all within walking distance.

The apartment had three bedrooms, a small kitchen, and an even smaller bathroom. There was no tub, but it did have a shower stall. As for the toilet, my knees crept under the sink whenever I was on it. No big deal. When the toilet stopped flushing two days after my arrival, that was more problematic.

One of the women I was living with had mentioned issues with the toilet. She hadn't gotten specific. Neither had she advised me of anything I should or shouldn't do. Consequently, I didn't know if I'd broken the toilet or one of my roommates did. All I knew was that it no longer flushed.

The water tank was all the way up at the ceiling, which was

higher than most. I couldn't reach the tank. I needed a ladder, but I had no idea where to get one. No one was home to ask.

What I also needed was to go to the bathroom. I couldn't wait until my roommates came back, especially since I didn't know when that might be. So, I improvised. Just as I had years before in Istanbul, when the water often didn't come on for two or three days at a time, I went to the kitchen and got a large pot. I then filled it with water and dumped it into the toilet, flushing manually. No problem. Been there, done that.

I would continue to be there doing that. I didn't know it at the time, but one roommate had left for an extended vacation, and the other worked strange, long hours at the airport. Like a ghost that moves things around to alert you to its presence but that you never actually see, I occasionally noticed signs the roommate had been in the apartment. But I didn't see her in person. What's more, she either never went to the bathroom or was so impressed with my workaround that she saw no need to fix the toilet.

We continued flushing with potfuls of water. For days. It wasn't that big a deal. I left the pot in the sink, and it simply became part of our routine.

Another part of my routine in Barcelona was a daily trip to the cybercafé. The apartment didn't have Internet, and it would be another year or two before cafés with Wi-Fi popped up everywhere.

The cybercafé was located in a commercial center on las Ramblas. Despite what the name suggested, there was no coffee. The café was little more than a bleak, windowless basement of rows and rows of computer terminals. Each was allotted its own area surrounded on three sides by privacy partitions. They were like study carrels, and there were hundreds of them. Even still, often there were scarcely enough to meet the demands of the endless succession of customers, at least half of whom were tourists. There were so many patrons that turnstiles had been installed at the front doors to control their comings and goings.

Barcelona is known for petty thievery. Tourists attract thieves. I knew to keep an extra close watch on my belongings when I was at the cybercafé. I always made sure to slip my backpack strap around my leg, even if no one was around.

Or, almost always.

I had just returned from a weekend trip to Montpellier, in the south of France. I hadn't been online for a couple of days, so I stopped by the Internet café on my way back to the apartment. The subterranean, fluorescent-lit facility was even more crowded than usual. Whereas ordinarily I got a seat next to a wall, making me less of a target, this time I had to sit in the middle of the room, at the end of an aisle.

After traveling for hours, I was tired of being confined by my backpack. I broke with my normal protocol and put the bag between my legs, instead of strapping it to one of them. Cradled in my crotch and surrounded by three walls, it would be fine.

A few emails later, I changed positions in the chair, casually bringing my legs together. Something didn't feel right. Then, a jolt of alarm: how could I put my legs together! Shouldn't something be in the way? Wasn't there a backpack between them?

I looked down.

Not anymore.

I panicked. What had happened to my backpack? Where was it? Who had taken it? I felt violated. I rushed to take a mental inventory of the backpack's contents.

How was it possible? The bag had been between my legs— a region generally known for its sensitivity. And what about the walls surrounding the cubicle? How had someone gotten around them?

I looked under the desk. The privacy partitions didn't extend to the floor; they were on top of the table, not below it. I thought my backpack had been walled in. I thought that enveloping it in a highly charged erogenous zone would afford it foolproof protection. Apparently there was a short circuit. My bag had been completely exposed.

I jumped out of my chair and rushed to the front desk. I was joined by three or four fellow victims. There wasn't just one thief at work. There were a few, and they had acted in unison. They had carried out a coordinated attack.

Not only were they successful, they were gone without a trace.

The toilet still not flushing, later that day I finally ran into one of my roommates. She promised to borrow a ladder from a neighbor. We could fix the toilet together that evening.

Excellent.

When I returned home again that night, not only was my roommate nowhere to be found, neither was the ladder. Maybe, I hoped, she had already fixed the toilet? Maybe she hadn't needed my help after all?

No such luck. I found the bathroom exactly as I had left it: pot in the sink, toilet out of commission.

I didn't mind flushing manually, but it did have certain disadvantages. If the water poured into the toilet at the wrong angle or with too much force, it splashed onto the floor or— even worse—sent toilet-bowl contents airborne.

No doubt that was why, after a couple of weeks of pot-flushing, one afternoon I returned home to find the bathroom smelled of bleach.

Well, then, where the hell was the ladder?

I would have preferred never to set foot in the cybercafé again. And I wouldn't, once I had finished spending my prepaid Internet credits.

When I returned the morning after my backpack was stolen, it was early enough that there weren't many customers.

I sat down at a computer next to a wall and slouched in my chair, making myself as inconspicuous as possible.

Shortly after, a young woman took a seat four or five computers over, at the end of my aisle. Once she got situated, she tossed her purse on the floor—leaving it wide open. It was even slightly behind her, out of her direct line of sight. Aghast at her carelessness, I burned with judgment. At least I had thought I was taking precautions the day before. She was practically begging to be robbed, her open purse enticing to thieves like blood to a shark.

Mere moments later, one was circling.

Even before I myself had been victimized, I'd paid enough attention to notice people who frequented the café who didn't seem to belong there. They were always young males, and they would sit down at a computer without logging on. They would then pretend to be online, while what they really did was survey their surroundings—presumably for an opportunity.

The anxious young man who now appeared sat down with his back to the woman at the end of my aisle. He was thin and of average height. He had hollow eyes and sharp cheek bones, his dark hair was oily. His expression etched into a grimace of disdain, he seemed like the sort of person who only smiled at someone else's suffering. Even better if he was responsible for it.

Soon, he hoped, he'd be grinning from ear to ear.

Focused on his target, he failed to pay much attention to me. It was a lazy oversight, almost as careless as the open purse. I pretended to look at my computer, though, in reality, I didn't take my eyes off him.

Without warning, with the speed and precision of someone who has honed their craft, his hand shot for the purse.

"¡*Ladrón!*" I yelled, alerting the entire café.

The woman turned to find herself face-to-face with the thief. She gasped, grabbing her purse. He recoiled, only to redirect his attention—and rage—at me. As he came for me, two men from the front desk—one standing over six feet tall and weighing more than two hundred pounds, much of it muscle—restrained him from behind.

I was just as, if not even more, enraged than the thief. Launching into an expletive-laden tirade that made use of nearly every insult I knew in Spanish, I gave voice to all the emotion I hadn't been able to express the day before. Whether or not he was the same thug who had stolen my backpack made no difference; in this context, they were all the same. Besides, even if he wasn't the one, in all likelihood he knew who was. He could pass along the message.

The thief was escorted out of the café. Beyond removing him from the premises, the staff didn't appear overly concerned. They didn't call the police. For a second, I wondered if they—staff and thieves alike—were all in on the scam. More likely, there were so many thieves committing so many petty thefts, the staff couldn't keep up. Same for the police, who no doubt had more pressing concerns.

I calmed down enough to spend my remaining credits. I then hightailed it out of the Internet crime den, never to set foot in it again.

A few days before my departure, the other roommate reappeared. It turned out she had not only taken a long vacation but spent time at her boyfriend's, followed by a few days on-site at her social services job. She asked about the pot in the bathroom. I explained the situation. In no time, her spry, fearless boyfriend had climbed on top of the bathroom sink and reattached whatever it was in the tank that needed to be reattached.

Nearly thirty days later, in just under thirty seconds, he had fixed the toilet.

I might have felt foolish, if standing on the sink didn't seem more so. I never would have trusted it to support my weight for long. Then again, I weighed more than the boyfriend did. Not only was he short, but he had the unnaturally thin body of a chain smoker. Regardless, at long last, the toilet had been fixed.

Or maybe not.

The next morning, as it does over and over again, history repeated itself. The boyfriend wasn't quite as ingenious as it seemed. Whatever he had reattached in the toilet tank had already come undone.

I went to the kitchen, got my pot, and picked back up where I had left off.

That might have been the end to the story, if the shower hadn't thrust itself onto center stage the morning of my departure.

Standing within the shower stall's narrow walls, I was only half awake, my mind wandering. The hot water felt good, soothing as it gently ushered my body back to life.

Until it turned ice cold.

It happened from one instant to the next. There was no warning. Neither was there anywhere to go to escape the water—the shower was too small. I reflexively grabbed the showerhead, ripped it from the wall mount, and held it to the side. My heart was racing, my breathing fast and shallow. Amidst a flurry of expletives, I tried to regain my composure.

I did. But the ordeal wasn't over.

My head was still covered in shampoo.

I tried to find a way to position myself so the least possible amount of water would get on my body. Icy cold spray stung my legs and torso, like lashes of a whip. There was no point. The shower was too small. I just had to do it.

I took another deep breath. Then, bending forward, I bit the bullet. I stuck my head under the water, submitting myself to its brutal chill. Rushing to rinse out the shampoo, I continued trying to get as little water as possible on my body. That proved the least of my concerns.

Instead, my undivided attention shifted to the water pelting my head, each drop like the icy tip of an arrow piercing its target. The water was so cold it felt like a vice grip on my skull, exerting a pressure that might crush it. I'd have a headache for days. A concussion was possible. If I stayed under the water much longer, brain damage was not out of the question.

Why had I even bothered to shower?

When I came out of the bathroom, as she struggled to keep a straight face, one of my roommates explained what had happened: the water heater had run out of propane during the final moments of my month in the apartment.

A backpack stolen from my crotch. A shower that nearly sent me into shock. In Barcelona I'd now found myself in the wrong place at the worst possible time not once, but twice. Though ordinarily not superstitious, I couldn't help but think of the old adage: bad things come in threes.

I rushed to finish packing my things, took one last pee—without stopping to fill the pot and flush—and headed for the train station.

8 A DAY AT THE BEACH

As soon as my Lebanese friend told me he'd finalized plans for his annual trip to Beirut, I knew this would be the year I joined him. I had another friend in the Levant whom I also wanted to visit. Michelle was living in Jerusalem, working with the United Nations to assess the impact of Israel's wall on West Bank communities. Apparently millions of dollars and years of analysis were necessary to establish that splitting communities in half had devastating effects.

Lebanon and Israel are notorious foes, countries between which it is impossible to travel as a tourist. Accordingly, I had chosen Amman, Jordan, as my entry point to the Middle East. From there, I would kick off my trip with a bus ride through the West Bank to Jerusalem. I prayed that wasn't analogous to saying I'd be starting my trip off with a bang.

After spending the night in Amman, I got a cab to the bus depot on the border. Despite being the only Westerner among hundreds of travelers, I felt welcome and at ease. No one directed any undesirable attention my way. Thanks to our shared experience, perhaps, I was just one more in the crowd. Busy with their own affairs, no one was concerned with mine.

When the time came to cross one of the most militarized zones in the world, everything changed. Expectation and tension were palpable. The transportation logistics were well organized, many crossings taking place each day. Nevertheless, there was a pervasive sense that anything could happen at any time. Departures could be delayed. Israel could decide to flex its muscle and close the border, reminding David who was Goliath. From one moment to the next, long-standing, deep-rooted tensions could erupt into something more sinister, as they had so many times before.

Hence the barbed wire and guard towers and, once we'd crossed the first checkpoint, space left intentionally blank. Empty desert. Breathing room where everyone held their breath. A buffer of nothing to ensure something came between the anger, hatred, and virulent mistrust simmering on both sides.

It was disheartening. It was eye-opening. It was unforgettable.

Until I spoke to Michelle.

I'd called to confirm that I would be arriving shortly.

"I have a boyfriend!" she exclaimed.

I had crossed the border without incident. Now I had a bombshell dropped on me.

For the entirety of our friendship, Michelle was looking for love. It always eluded her. Apparently her luck had changed.

"I didn't want to tell you, because I wanted to make sure it was the real thing. And now I know it is. He's here with me, so you'll meet him when you get here!"

How had I spent my morning? What had I just experienced? It no longer mattered, all of it rendered a blur. Michelle had a boyfriend! And it was serious! She was in love!

Who was the lucky man? What did he look like? What would he be like?

The answer to that last question would prove painfully simple.

He'd be full of surprises.

Michelle was waiting for me when I stepped off the bus in Jerusalem. There were hugs and squeals of delight and more hugs.

There was also Sameer.

Sameer was an Arab Israeli in his late thirties. Taken individually, his prominent nose; large, widely spaced eyes; and high forehead were all a little quirky. Taken as a whole, they somehow came together to form a handsome mug. He had an athletic, medium-sized frame, but he looked taller than he was. His limbs were long and toned, his body strong and lithe. He might have been almost graceful, if it weren't for his erratic energy.

It started the moment we met. Sameer could not stop smiling at me. He couldn't stop touching me, either, putting his arm over my shoulder as though we were old friends. The fact we had only just met didn't matter: I was an amazing friend. He told me so over and over.

At first, like a puppy dog that doesn't know any better, it was endearing. But even puppies eventually calm down. Sameer showed no sign of relenting. We went for coffee. We took an excursion to a lookout with a panoramic view of the Old City, the Dome of the Rock shining like a piece of sun fallen to earth. All the while, Sameer kept at it, showering me with effusive praise. Michelle grew almost as uncomfortable as I was. Finally, she intervened.

"Sameer," she laughed nervously, his arm once again wrapped around me, a boa slowly constricting. "I think Matthew knows that you're glad he's here."

"But I am!" he insisted, squeezing me tighter. "What a great guy!"

And so it went for the rest of the day.

Sameer was sweet. He meant well. He was trying way too hard.

The last thing I needed was someone clinging to me. It was summertime in Israel. It was infernally hot and unbearably humid. Every time Sameer put his arm around me, my saturated shirt stuck to my flesh, another rivulet of sweat streaming down my back. I had long struggled with athlete's foot; I now feared an outbreak of athlete's body. Circumstances were ripe for a massive fungal outbreak.

But that wasn't the real issue. The real issue was that Sameer was so inexplicably taken by me the instant I stepped off the bus. I like to think I'm a likable guy. I like to think I make a good first impression. Neither could possibly account for Sameer's unbridled enthusiasm.

I tried to tell myself that his over-the-top welcome was, at least partially, cultural. I knew better. I have close friends who are Arabs. I've lived with them and celebrated their holidays and helped them welcome their own visitors. I have met many others on my travels. I wasn't some sort of expert; but neither was I a stranger to their customs.

It wasn't cultural. It was Sameer.

That evening Michelle and I headed to Tel Aviv, where she had rented a studio near the beach for the summer. Sameer stayed in Jerusalem. He had to work the next day. Michelle and I would not be alone for long, however—I wasn't the only San Franciscan coming to visit. Her friend Rachel joined us in Tel Aviv the next day.

Michelle and I had gone to the beach that morning. Now, with Rachel at our side, we played tourist. We visited the old Arab town of Jaffa. We had a late lunch at a hip cafe with a shaded courtyard, perused the offerings of a succession of street vendors, and returned to Michelle's studio to rest. When the sun began its colorful descent over the Mediterranean, we headed back out, taking a leisurely stroll in an animated part of town we hadn't yet visited.

We topped off our day with a long dinner under the stars. It was a balmy summer night, the restaurant festive, the air sultry. We ate too much. We drank even more. We laughed our asses off, savoring the fact we had come together so far from home. It felt decadent to sit outside in shorts and a t-shirt, particularly being from San Francisco. We relished it. At home, nightfall usually meant jeans and sweatshirts, protective layers against damp fog and chilly breezes. Here it meant relief from the day, from its scorching heat and blinding light. Nighttime was liberation. It was cause for celebration. And celebrate we did.

The sights we saw.

The adventures we had.

The laughter we shared.

All of it made a lasting impression. And yet, as memorable as was our first full day together, it was the following that I'll never forget.

None of us will.

Sameer was able to get the day off, something in doubt until the very last minute. So, he and Michelle decided to do something special: we were going to the Dead Sea. On our way to the West Bank, we'd stop at Masada, one of Judaism's most sacred sites. Afterwards, we'd spend the afternoon at the beach, floating effortlessly in the Dead Sea's buoyant waters and covering ourselves head to toe in its famous mud. Revered the world over for its skincare benefits, the mud was sure to provide the rejuvenation for which my sun-damaged, spotty complexion had long cried out. I could hardly wait to bask in my renewed glow.

Michelle tried to convince Sameer to end the day in Jericho. He categorically refused. He wouldn't even consider it. He might have been Arab, but his license plates betrayed the fact he was also Israeli. He feared the Palestinians would throw rocks at his car.

"I cross over to the West Bank every day," Michelle admonished. "Israelis don't just drive over to Jericho to hang out. People would assume we're aid workers or tourists. It would be fine."

Sameer wouldn't budge. I was disappointed. All my money

was being spent on the other side of the wall, the same side where millions of my country's tax dollars flowed nonstop every day like oil through a pipeline. I would have liked to spread the wealth, to make even the smallest contribution to the wellbeing of those isolated on the wrong side of the wall. My tax dollars had helped pay for that, too.

Besides, I was curious to visit a West Bank town. Flying through the Occupied Territories on the bus had been interesting, but my experience had been limited to what I could see from the window. It was sort of like claiming to have visited a country just because I'd been in its airport. I'd seen it through the glass, but I couldn't in good conscience claim to have been there.

Jericho, in particular, intrigued me. It was one of the oldest continuously inhabited cities in the world. The Mount of Temptation was on its outskirts, traditionally considered where Jesus faced off with the Devil. I was frustrated to know I would be so close without being able to see it. Jesus had long since moved on, but much about the area must have reminded the Devil of home—if nothing else, it was hot as Hell.

We packed the car for a day at the beach, and headed out.

Prior to my trip to the Middle East, I had hoped to make it to the Dead Sea. I hadn't been sure it would work out. Now we were on our way, and I was excited. The sky was a bright blue, the sun at its most radiant. The desert scenery was severe: sandy, rocky expanses with little vegetation. It, too, was beautiful.

Off on the sides of the highway, occasional Bedouin shepherds tended flocks that somehow survived in the desolate landscape. Did the sheep eat stones? Could they digest dust? I wondered, too, how the shepherds survived alongside the modern thoroughfares parsing up their lands and in the shadows of the settlements quickly overtaking them.

Masada was impressive, situated atop an isolated rock plateau with edges that plummeted 1300 feet. The word Masada means "fortress." An island in the sky, it was easy to see why the site had been an obvious choice for an ancient stronghold. Its strength, however, was also its weakness. Masada's glory days ended when the Romans surrounded it, and 960 of its rebel inhabitants committed suicide.

If we had felt more adventurous, we could have set off at dawn for the traditional hike to the top. We were all hikers, and ordinarily we would have been up for the challenge. Today, though, Masada was just the first of two stops. Despite being one of Israel's most visited sites, for us it wasn't the main attraction. We took the easy way up. Dangling from cables high above the desert floor, we made the ascent in an air-conditioned gondola.

As if to celebrate our arrival at the top, Sameer busted out a bottle of beer. I was surprised. I hadn't realized he had beer in his backpack. And it wasn't even lunchtime. All the same, we were in the desert. It was early, but it was already hot. Assuming the beer was still cold, it made sense.

The ruins were extensive. Once upon a time, there had been palaces, towers, and gates. Barracks, storerooms, and cisterns. A synagogue and, even, a Byzantine church. Today all was reduced to little more than a maze of stone walls. Meandering stairs, suspended walkways, and jaw-dropping overlooks guided us from one site to another.

Even more impressive were the views. We were surrounded by arid mountains. The Dead Sea was in plain sight. Between us and it, total desolation, the barren terrain unimaginably dry. Desert at its most severe. The tormented crust of the Earth seemed to be gasping for breath, struggling under a thick haze, as if the rock itself were evaporating. From our perspective high above, the vast panorama seemed lifeless, ravaged by seismic upheaval, by intolerable heat and an absolute absence of water. The sea was right there, but it was exceptionally saline; it could offer no relief to the parched landscape on its shores.

The longer we stayed outside, the hotter it got, the more a

trip to the beach appealed. Before we could get back into the gondola, though, Sameer had to polish off a beer. We'd been exploring the ruins for a couple of hours. Was he still nursing the same bottle, or had he moved onto another? Not that it mattered. It was just curious, particularly given no one else was drinking.

Heading back down in the gondola, we reveled in the cool air. Sameer was even more animated than usual. Clearly he had found the ruins not only inspiring, but energizing, like too much espresso. He made jokes that didn't quite translate. He was touchy feely, mostly with Michelle, but with Rachel and me, as well. He couldn't stop moving, fidgeting nervously. He was so full of life, in fact, that when we got to the car, Michelle took the keys.

She would drive.

Our Dead Sea "resort" consisted of little more than a parking lot, bathrooms, and a concession stand. There were also outdoor showers. It was basic, but completely adequate for our needs. We were just there for the mud.

There was a fair number of other beachgoers, but it wasn't crowded. After walking down a hill a short distance from the entrance, we found a small section of beach with an unclaimed shelter. Grateful for the shade, we snagged the spot, put down our things, and stripped to our swimming suits. Sameer and Rachel pulled a couple of beers out of the cooler we'd brought along, while Michelle and I got some snacks out of the bags. It wasn't long before we were in the water. Looking back at the shore, I observed a lifeguard keeping vigilant watch from a more populated area a little further down the beach.

I had long heard that floating in the Dead Sea was almost effortless, because of its exceptionally high salt content. It was true. It was also funny to experience. Like a helium balloon on the air, my body rose out of the water. Submerging myself took more effort than staying afloat. This water looked the same as any other; clearly, it was not. Laughing like children, we played in it, we thrashed around and splashed each other with it, taking delight in the novelty.

Eventually we returned to shore. Lunch followed. After, another dip in the sea.

"Let's piss off the lifeguard," Sameer proposed, as we waded back into the water. Apparently the meal had not only reenergized but emboldened him.

No one said anything. Rachel and I looked at Michelle.

"Sameer," she began playfully, like a mother pretending to be a good sport when what she's really doing is trying to talk her child out of something reckless. "I don't think that's a good idea."

It genuinely wasn't. Sameer may have been an Israeli citizen, but he had been discharged from the army under less than favorable circumstances. I couldn't help but think that being an Arab with a questionable military record made him a very poor candidate for a run-in with the authorities.

He didn't care.

"Come on, you guys! Let's go!"

He plunged back into the water, swimming straight for Jordan, in sight in the distance. Had I known two days earlier that swimming was an option, I might have saved myself the bus ticket.

Much to my surprise, Michelle and Rachel joined Sameer in his initiative to instigate an international border incident. Like a child tempted by peer pressure, but unable to go through with something he knows is wrong, I stayed behind. I was still struggling to figure out why provoking an Israeli lifeguard was not only a good idea but so much fun. I kept imagining the young lifeguard picking up an Uzi and blowing Sameer out of the water for his ill-conceived prank.

Once Sameer got far enough from shore, sure enough, the lifeguard began blowing his whistle. Thankfully, he did not fire up his Uzi.

Sameer laughed and yelled some things I didn't understand. Mission accomplished, he didn't go any further. Michelle and

Rachel had feigned being on board, but hadn't followed Sameer all the way out. Their bikinis didn't have pockets; I wondered if one of them had second thoughts when she remembered she wasn't carrying her passport. It was also possible they had both realized that intentionally creating conflict in a world-infamous conflict zone was about as smart as joking about having a bomb on a plane. Treading water, they looked at each other, laughing nervously.

Sameer and the gals messed around in the water for a bit, before coming back to shore.

It was time to play in the mud.

Digging into the shoreline, we scooped up moist clay and applied coat after coat to our skin, our bodies canvasses for one another's hands. It didn't take long before we had all achieved that unmistakable Dead Sea look: we looked like drowned zombies. Laughs were had. Photos were taken. Then we lay down on the beach.

Applying the mud was just the first step. For full effect, it had to dry in the sun. Only then could it be rinsed off, revealing skin so silky it was sure to be the envy of baby butts the world over.

In 100-degree temperatures, it doesn't take long for mud to dry. Like pottery in a kiln, we were all soon cooked to perfection, our extra layer of skin beginning to crack. The women wanted to bask in the sun a little longer. Sameer and I headed up to the outdoor showers.

Four showerheads were mounted on arms branching off from a single pole. We were in the middle of the common area, near the entrance. There were people everywhere.

When Sameer and I arrived, there were also two little boys at the showers. I assumed they were brothers. The older not more than ten or eleven, the other was probably a year or two younger. I acknowledged each with a smile, and began washing off my mud.

Sameer began washing off, too. He also began mumbling to himself. Once again, it was odd. Still, given his erratic behavior over the course of the day, I didn't think much of it.

When he grunted something to one of the boys, I was surprised. Sameer's tone seemed aggressive, even mean. The brief exchange was in Arabic, however, so I couldn't understand what he said. My suspicions were confirmed when I looked at the boy: he, too, seemed taken aback, looking at Sameer with mistrust. His feelings might have even been hurt. Sameer didn't say anything else.

Instead, he took off his Speedo.

My jaw dropped.

Before I let my emotions get away from me, I caught myself. Maybe it was OK? Sameer was the local. He was the one who should know what was and was not culturally acceptable—even if he was a little out of it.

I was an American, after all. My knee-jerk reaction to nudity was bound to be prudish. In a culture that has begun espousing vaginal rejuvenation and even finds fault with our anuses, which we're now told look better bleached, we can be forgiven our distorted views—if not outright fear—of the human form.

Other cultures aren't nearly as unforgiving. The West Bank was a far cry from the Cote d'Azur; but maybe slipping off swim trunks while showering wasn't that big a deal? Sand got up into cracks on this beach, just as much as on any other. And we were at the beach, after all. If there was anyplace it was acceptable for the body to be on display, even in a more traditional society, this would be it. I could imagine how Sameer taking off his swimsuit might not be that big a deal.

What followed, however, was a very big one.

Sameer reached up to the chain dangling from the showerhead, the one used to start and stop the flow of water. Hanging from it with one arm, he then began a series of impassioned pelvic thrusts. Seemingly mistaking the shower pipe for a stripper pole, he flopped his genitalia up and down, his hips gyrating, his wiener waving, his balls bouncing. Having suffered all day in sweaty silence, they celebrated their freedom. Unleashed, they went wild.

A laugh escaped me. But it wasn't a normal laugh. It was the kind of laugh that erupts when you're caught off guard. It was the kind of laugh that happens when you get news so horrible you reflexively hide your feelings. You laugh so you don't cry; you laugh because you need a moment to process what you've just been told.

I looked at the boy closer to Sameer. His jaw had dropped. His eyes had grown large.

I looked beyond the shower, toward the concession area. I saw Muslim women dressed in hijabs.

No. My gut reaction was the right reaction. This was not supposed to be happening. Sameer was not supposed to be doing this. This was not Ibiza. We were far from Esalen. Nudity was not acceptable here.

Never mind jiggling genitalia.

I looked at the little boy again. He was backing away from the shower.

I did not want to end up in a West Bank jail.

I bolted.

Rushing down the hill to our stretch of beach, I called out to Michelle.

"I don't know how to tell you this, but ..." I began, catching my breath. I then told her what had happened.

Michelle was mortified.

"Here he comes," said Rachel, her expression betraying her own shock.

Michelle and I turned to look. Sure enough, muttering to himself, Sameer was strolling down the hill, towel over his shoulder. Unlike the last time I had seen him, he was wearing his bathing suit. Like escaped animals forced back into their cage, his testicles must have resented their return to captivity.

As Sameer approached, he didn't look us in the eyes. Instead, still saying things to himself in Arabic, he grabbed a beer. He then wandered to the end of our section of beach.

Michelle didn't know what to say. So, for the time-being,

she said nothing. Confused and upset, she and Rachel headed to the showers.

They were leaving me alone with him?

As they vanished up the slope, I looked down the beach.

Sameer was doing handstands. Or, rather, Sameer was trying to do handstands. Whether drunk, drugged, or suffering some sort of mental breakdown, his coordination was a little off. Losing his balance again and again, soon he was covered in sand.

At least I didn't have to talk to him. He didn't even know I was there.

Michelle and Rachel may have left me alone with Sameer, but they didn't dillydally at the showers. They knew we were in crisis mode. What they didn't know—what none of us had time to anticipate—was that the crisis was about to escalate.

When they returned, we began packing up our things to go. Sameer was still at the end of the beach. He had yet to perfect his handstand, but he continued amusing himself and muttering nonsense. As far as I could tell, his genitalia had not found their way back to freedom.

"Oh shit, you guys," I said. Michelle and Rachel had their backs turned to the hill. "Don't look now, but security's coming. And a man. And one of the boys from the shower."

Another look of horror washed over Michelle's face. None of us moved, other than to direct our attention to our fast-approaching guests.

We weren't the ones they wanted to talk to. Rushing past us as though we weren't even there, the security guard, father, and older boy went straight for Sameer.

The conversation took place in Arabic. Except it wasn't a conversation. Instead, from one moment to the next, Sameer became a raging madman, yelling at the top of his lungs. He was insane. He had genuinely lost it. Watching him was not only disturbing, it was frightening.

"Sameer!" Michelle yelled, rushing over to him. "Sameer, stop! What are you doing? Stop!"

Sameer continued lashing out. The men didn't engage.

Instead, now clear about what they were up against, without another word, they turned and beat a hasty retreat back up the hill.

"What the hell was that!" Michelle cried. She was livid.

Sameer said nothing, dismissing her concerns with a wave of his hand.

All of us in shock, we packed our things in silence. We then began the slow march up the slope, Sameer several steps ahead of us. He seemed embarrassed. But he also still seemed out of it. We didn't know what he might do next. Naked cartwheels? Hump a beach ball? Pick a fight with a security guard? He had already proven anything was possible. We gave him space.

"This isn't over, you guys," I warned Michelle and Rachel, lowering my voice. "This is not over."

When we got to the top of the hill, Sameer went to the bathroom. It seemed like a bad idea to let him go alone, but I sure as hell wasn't going in with him. Michelle and Rachel had to make a pit stop, too. I waited outside, scanning the surroundings. People came and went, men and women, boys and girls. Customers ordered refreshments at the concession stand. Bathers washed off mud at the scene of the crime, oblivious to what had transpired shortly before. It all seemed so innocent, just another day at the beach.

I kept watching, convinced a battalion of security was going to show up at any moment.

This was not over.

Everyone came out of the bathroom. Sameer was still wearing his bathing suit. Good. No one had run screaming out of the bathroom while he was inside. Even better.

I looked around as we headed toward the exit. When were we going to be stopped?

My heart beating fast, I glanced at the security guard at the gate. He looked at us, saying something into his walkie-talkie. I braced for the inevitable.

It didn't happen.

Instead, we walked right through the gate. We continued all the way to the car. I kept looking around, waiting, expecting.

My mind raced.

We put our things in the trunk.

We got into the car, without a word.

We drove off.

Nothing.

They had let us go?

I was dumbfounded. All I could think was that the security officers had decided to take the path of least resistance. They just wanted us out of there.

Still, it didn't feel right. I could not believe it was that simple. And yet, apparently it was. We had left. We were on the road, on our way home. It was hard to believe, but that's what was happening.

Michelle was at the wheel. Sameer was in the passenger seat. I sat behind him, Rachel at my side.

Out of harm's way, Sameer found his voice again. Launching into a vicious, rambling diatribe, he vented his disgust that Michelle had tried to intervene on the beach.

"You Western women are all the same!" he hissed, becoming more aggressive.

Until then, Sameer had portrayed himself as progressively minded and spiritually aware. The episode at the showers. His rage on the beach. The ugly truths bursting to the surface now. I didn't care how many hours a day he meditated or how much he practiced yoga or gratitude or loving kindness. He wasn't nearly as far along the path to enlightenment as he might have liked to think.

If, say, instead of Sameer, Pema Chodron had been in the passenger seat, it's hard to imagine I would have found myself assessing whether it would be easier to pull off a strangle hold or a headlock on her from the backseat. Yet that's what I now found myself doing: plotting how to restrain Sameer, if it came to that. The more he got in Michelle's face, the more he gesticulated at her wildly, the more I feared he was about to cause her physical harm.

As it turned out, my fears were unwarranted. I wouldn't have to restrain Sameer. Someone else would take care of that for me.

Sirens sounded behind us.

I was right. We weren't getting away so easily. We had just been waiting for the police.

We pulled over. The officers asked Sameer to step out of the car. They took him to theirs for questioning.

Michelle, Rachel, and I waited. No one said anything.

An officer returned to our car. Without Sameer. They were taking him back to the resort. We needed to follow.

"Michelle, I'm really sorry," I began, as we headed back to the beach. "But if they question me, I'm going to have to be honest about what happened."

Not only was I looking out for myself, I was thinking of the boys. I was not going to lie to protect Sameer from what he had done in front of them.

Back at the resort, Rachel and I sat at one table, Sameer and Michelle sat at another, at a distance. On the other side of the concession area, the two boys sat with their family. The police officers walked back and forth between them and Sameer, documenting the facts and comparing stories.

I was on edge for the duration, downing water like I might have shots of whisky. Every time the police finished a round of questioning, I couldn't help but think I would be next.

I never was.

It took a couple of hours, but the police eventually reached a verdict.

Sameer was headed to jail.

I was much less concerned about him, than I was about Michelle. Miraculously, she was able to hold it together. Part of it was the responsibility she felt toward us, her guests; part of it was the disgust she felt toward Sameer, both for what he'd done and for getting us into the situation.

"You guys, I am so, so sorry," she said, walking over, after Sameer was handcuffed and escorted off the premises.

Rachel and I were quick to reassure her that, whatever it was that had just happened—we were still trying to make sense of it all—it was not her fault.

We made our way back to the car.

"You know," said Michelle, an unexpected smile forming on her lips, the first we'd seen for hours. "There is at least one good thing that came of all this."

"What do you mean?" I asked.

"Sameer's not here," Michelle replied, expecting Rachel and me to make some sort of connection.

"OK," said Rachel, waiting for the follow-up.

"We can go to Jericho!"

Jericho is a town of about 20,000 people. As we drove into the center, a Palestinian soldier who seemed to be directing traffic looked into our car. When he saw we were tourists, a huge grin spread across his face. He gave us the thumbs up. I felt a pang of emotion.

The town was centered around a palm-filled square, two- and three-story buildings facing it on all sides, including a town hall. An otherwise simple building, three tall arches over the entryway gave it an air of authority. In the square itself, I was surprised by the number of taxis. They were everywhere, both circling and parked. The town was small. There weren't many people. Why did they need so many taxis?

We easily found a parking space on a street just off the square. Rachel wrapped a scarf around her shoulders out of respect for the local sensibilities. We then set off to find a place to eat. It didn't take long.

The owner and his teenage son were surprised to see us. The former was a rotund, balding fellow in his fifties. He wore a white button-down shirt and dark slacks. No surprise that beads of sweat had gathered on his forehead, along with damp patches under his arms. Wearing jeans and a t-shirt, his son seemed more comfortable. He was skinny as a rail and all smiles.

The restaurant was empty. I couldn't help but wonder how often they had customers. Did people in the West Bank have disposable income for meals out? We'd seen many signs on the drive into town referencing foreign aid from European countries and the United States. I knew that Israel sometimes shut down the border, putting a financial strangle hold on the Occupied Territories. Given all that, it was hard to imagine a thriving services industry. Then again, even in the poorest places, there are always people with money.

After the warmest of welcomes, we were shown upstairs to an outdoor terrace. With our pick of tables, we chose one overlooking the square. The owner and his son were as mystified as they were grateful to have us there. Not only did they ask the typical questions, such as where we were from, but they were curious about what had brought us to Jericho. Michelle explained her work with the United Nations. For some reason she neglected to mention that our visit wouldn't have been possible if her boyfriend hadn't exposed himself at the Dead Sea and been apprehended by the Israeli authorities.

I wondered how his interrogation was going.

Our table was soon covered with all the Arab favorites and then some: hummus, baba ghanouj, and falafel; pickled vegetables, fresh salads, and cooked dishes whose names I didn't catch. There were piles of pitas, a mound of french fries, and a tall bottle of water, standing at the ready to wash it all down.

The people. The welcome. The food. All of it was incredible.

Our bodies well-nourished, it was time to devote some attention to our souls.

After taking leave of our hosts, we got back into the car and headed to the outskirts of town. No one was at the Mount of Temptation when we arrived. There was no sign of Satan either, though a group of monks could scarcely have left a bigger mark. Centuries earlier, they had built a monastery into the mountainside.

A large placard indicated that the site fell under the aegis of the Palestinian National Authority's Ministry of Tourism and Antiquities. Palestine had a Ministry of Tourism? Then again,

Bethlehem was in Palestine—not exactly a minor tourist draw.

Other than the monastery, the Mount itself was essentially a big, barren rock. Had we arrived earlier, we could have taken our second cable car ride of the day up to the top.

Turning back toward the valley, we saw Jericho in the distance. Michelle mentioned that it was almost 1000 feet below sea level, making it the lowest city in the world. Closer at hand was barren agricultural land that seemed to have fallen into disuse, or maybe the growing season had already passed. Some deep-green bushes in a plot alongside the road seemed strikingly out of place. Less surprising were tall palms that popped up here and there, they, too, doing their part to enliven the severe desert landscape.

After we snapped a few pics, our clandestine excursion to Jericho came to an end. The car had made it through the entire adventure without a scratch. Either we'd been really lucky, or Sameer's fears had been unfounded. Ironic that *he* had been so worried about us being victimized.

As for his own crimes—or, at least, his serious indiscretions—he didn't spend the night in jail. He would, however, spend the next couple of years explaining himself in court. His case was never formally closed, but it did eventually run its course. The system essentially lost interest.

Michelle and Sameer are still together, living in the United States.

They spend very little time at the beach.

9 FALLING TO PIECES

I wanted to hide out from the world. I wanted to focus on writing. I wanted to lose myself in nature. When online I discovered a tiny, dirt-cheap house in an isolated mountain village in southern Spain, I knew I'd found exactly what I was looking for. I had just arrived, and the landlords, a gay British couple who lived down on the coast, were giving me a tour.

When we got to the bathroom, something stood out right away. It wasn't the room's minuscule size or unusually low ceiling or lack of windows, all of which made it feel like a cave. It was the boulder sticking out of the wall. Perhaps four feet tall and three feet wide, in a room barely large enough for one person, the boulder was hard to miss.

It wasn't a decorative element. At least not a deliberate one. It was part of the mountainside on which the village was built. Too large to be easily removed, the boulder had been left where it was, the house constructed around it. The fact the building originally had been a stable no doubt made the boulder even less of an issue. Village archives showed no record of donkeys, goats, or chickens lodging any formal complaints about the big rock sticking out of the wall.

As interesting as it was visually, something else set the boulder apart.

It was alive.

I was never able to explain it. Somehow little pieces of rock routinely fell from the boulder, gathering at its base like drops of water that go unnoticed until enough of them form a pool. I couldn't help but wonder if the big rock wasn't crying softly to itself as it slowly fell to pieces. I didn't know what to do, other than be there for it, which I was, several times a day.

That's because the toilet was right next it. Like the boulder, it, too, was under the staircase. If you were a man (or, for that matter, an adventuresome woman), you were welcome to attempt peeing standing up. However, doing so required that you lean forward at a 45-degree angle and balance yourself against the wall. The underside of the staircase was so low that standing upright was nearly impossible.

The encroaching staircase did have one advantage. If you dozed off while on the pot, you didn't have far to fall before hitting your head on the stairs, guaranteeing that you woke up before tumbling to the floor. When it happened to me, late one night after a few too many glasses of wine, I couldn't have been more thankful the stairs were there to stop my fall.

The bathroom had a small shower. It even had a shower curtain, hung from a tree branch (I could never decide if it was charmingly rustic or, well, sort of pathetic). It also had very hot water and a place to hang the showerhead. Compared to some of the other bathing facilities on my travels, it was full service.

There was, however, one thing that bothered me about the shower: I wasn't the only one using it.

In all fairness, they were there before me. On the other hand, I was the one paying the rent. And I didn't appreciate how they snuck around, only showing up at night—and hoping I wouldn't notice. It felt deceitful. And intrusive. What's more, it wasn't just once in a while. It was every night, without fail. If I turned on the lights, they were there, caught in the act, doing whatever it was they did under the cover of darkness. Worst of all, there were lots of them.

Cockroaches.

In addition to the shower drain, I suspected they came up

through the kitchen sink, since they were sure to be found on the kitchen floor, too, whenever I went downstairs at night. What I was never able to figure out was whether there were three different species or a single variety in different stages of its lifecycle.

Never a big fan of toxic chemicals, it was only after exhausting all my options that I finally bought the bug spray. I had given the little house a deep cleaning. I had made sure never to leave so much as a crumb on the countertops or floor. I had hoped my presence—my moving around and turning the lights on and off as I went about my business—would act as a deterrent. But the roaches were already well established. They weren't going anywhere. They simply changed their habits, like rebellious youth, waiting until I went to bed to come out and party.

The chemicals reduced their numbers. However, the bug spray in the shower washed away each time I bathed. The largest, most unsightly creatures continued making their routine appearances through the drain.

Until I shut them out.

I didn't need chemicals, at least not in the shower. I needed a barricade. When I discovered that the coffee cups in the kitchen fit perfectly over the shower drain, I had my solution.

Each morning before I showered, I tapped the coffee cup several times, signaling to any roaches still trying to breach my defenses that they needed to be on their way. I was reclaiming the shower for myself.

One morning, still half asleep, I went downstairs, tapped on the coffee cup, and picked it up. Lying in wait, a huge roach made a break for it, scurrying into the shower. Caught off guard, I dropped the coffee cup and jumped back.

It wasn't that I was unaccustomed to roaches. Besides the ones in the house, I had encountered lots of them on my travels. Some of those encounters had made more of an impression than others—but none stood out more than Palm Springs.

A friend had purchased a condo, and she needed someone to drive down some things for the new place. She would bring a second load in a separate car the next day. Never having been to Palm Springs, I was more than happy to do her the favor, especially since I was getting a free trip out of the deal.

After a seven-hour drive from San Francisco, I easily found the condo, located in a stucco-covered, seventies-era complex, an all-too-familiar agglomeration of uninspired cream-colored boxes and labyrinthine parking lots. I let myself in and headed for the bathroom. Turning on the light, I discovered roach carcasses littering the tub and sink. I took the fact that they were all dead—and seemed to have been for quite a while—as a sign the apartment had been treated by exterminators, and hoped for the best.

Nearly midnight, I got settled in the apartment, unrolled my sleeping bag on the floor, and turned out the lights. I was exhausted. The floor was hard, but lying down and stretching out felt good.

As I drifted off to sleep, I heard the faint sound of a television in a neighboring unit. I couldn't tell where the sound was coming from exactly. Most likely it was from downstairs.

The more I listened—in spite of myself, since I was trying to fall asleep—the more I began to question what I heard. The sounds seemed vaguely electronic, but I gradually became less certain they were coming from a television, after all.

I felt something on my head.

Mussing my hair as though I'd mistaken depilatory cream for shampoo and had to rinse it out before every follicle was burnt from my head, I jumped up and turned on the light. A large roach was scrambling across the floor. No furnishings to afford it any cover, I saw the filth-loving creature in all its vile glory: jagged legs; useless, folded wings; and long, probing antennae.

It hadn't been a TV. It had been a roach. On my head.

So close I had heard its peculiar mumbling.

Who even knew roaches mumbled?
I rolled up my sleeping bag and went to find a hotel.

As for the roach now in my shower, it was about three inches long. There wasn't room in the bathroom for the both of us. One of us had to go.

I ran to the kitchen, grabbed the broom, and went to battle. The black insect darted up and down the white walls of the shower. Over and over I swatted with the broom, my adrenaline pumping. Over and over the roach narrowly escaped. Even when I did make contact, the defiant bug withstood the impact without injury (having no bones has its advantages). More than once, I could have sworn I even heard it laugh.

So, not only did roaches mumble, they laughed, too?

Despite its defiance, ultimately the roach was no less happy with the situation than I. Eventually conceding defeat, it bolted for the drain. I rushed to turn on the shower, hoping to make the drainpipe into a waterslide, washing the brazen beast that much further away, down the mountain, ideally, if not all the way out to sea.

Could roaches swim?

From that day forward, my morning taps on the coffee cup were considerably more emphatic than prior to the face-off. At times I got so carried away they seemed to reverberate to the house's very foundation, if not the base of the mountain. In any event, I had made my point. My creepy, crawly adversary never again showed its beady-eyed face.

10 REARVIEW MIRROR

My friend Arolynn and her partner Bill had just moved from Maine to Tucson. Both in their mid-seventies, they had not only bought a new house but opened an ice cream store—or, *parlor*, as Arolynn called it in her distinctive Maine accent. She'd never lost it, despite years living in the Bay Area, which was where our mutual friend Liz and I had met her. Over a decade earlier, we had all worked together in downtown San Francisco.

The new business venture was how Arolynn and Bill intended to both spend and fund their Golden Years. Liz and I not only wanted to support their new endeavor, but see the new house. Liz assumed we would fly; I suggested we drive. After an exceptionally wet spring, the desert was an awesome spectacle of color. If the pictures online were to be believed, the entire landscape was one big super bloom. We would stop in Joshua Tree en route, and Mojave on the way back.

Although they had to work at the parlor for most of our stay, Arolynn and Bill were able to take one full day off. Leaving our rental behind, we headed off in their car to make the most of our day together.

As we passed through rolling hills of golden grasses and flatlands of barren desert, that emblematic, quintessential cactus, the Saguaro, stood with arms upraised. We ventured almost all the way to the Mexican border, where we visited a national park with expansive mountaintop views and stunning rock formations. We stopped by a small town, where a historic hotel surprised us with a priceless—and immense—mural of antique Tiffany glass. We had dinner in another town, this one right out of the Wild West, complete with dusty roads, raucous saloons, and a corral so famous it had made it into the history books (and now charged admission). After a full day of our usual lively banter and meaningful conversation, we returned home late into the night.

As we pulled up to the house, I got out of Arolynn and Bill's car. The rental Liz and I had driven from San Francisco, a midsize, silver Mazda, was parked in front of the garage. I needed to move it, so Bill could put their car inside.

I got into the rental and rolled down the window. The Mazda had been sitting in the sun since morning; the air inside was stuffy and smelled synthetic, as if the interior plastics had been exhaling toxins all day. I couldn't move the car yet, because Bill had me blocked in. I waited.

Liz had walked up the driveway and was standing in front of the garage, her full blond hair aglow in the lamplight. A backpack was slung over her shoulder, and a bag of leftovers from our picnic earlier sat at her feet. Looking back at Bill and Arolynn, she seemed perplexed. I peered into my rearview mirror, trying to get a sense for what was going on. For some reason, Bill and Arolynn had also both gotten out of the car. I caught glimpses of them moving between darkness and light, but my view was mostly obstructed by their vehicle.

I turned back to Liz. She shot me a look of confusion, before again diverting her gaze toward the street. She didn't seem to understand what was happening either. I tried to be patient, the car running.

"Do not move!" Bill yelled.

My eyes darted to the rearview mirror. Bill had his hands raised, palms upturned in a universal gesture that again commanded me not to move. He was overcome by panic.

What was wrong?

I had no plans to move. The other car was still parked behind me, and neither Arolynn nor Bill was in it. I wasn't going anywhere—I couldn't go anywhere, not even if I wanted to. Why did Bill feel the need to insist I stay put? What was he afraid of? And where was Arolynn? A moment earlier I'd seen her white locks go down, below my line of sight. They had yet to come back up.

My eyes returned to Liz. Without warning, she covered her mouth, caught off guard by something she had just seen— something I could not. She burst into laughter, an expression of disbelief overtaking her face.

"What!" I called out, begging her to clue me in.

Liz tried to say something, but stopped short. Once again she was distracted. And she was laughing too hard.

The odd man out, I looked into my rearview mirror yet again, my only window onto the mysterious events unfolding so close but so far away. I still saw nothing, other than a few lights in the darkness and the back of Bill's head. What was he looking at? And speaking of heads, where was Arolynn's? Like a seal disappearing underwater for a small eternity, it hadn't resurfaced.

"Don't move!" Bill shouted again, turning to make sure I hadn't had second thoughts and decided to pull out of the driveway, smashing into his car and flattening both him and Arolynn.

If somebody didn't tell me what was happening, I just might.

Instead, I continued waiting, the car still idling. Should I turn it off? While I was at it, should I get out and go see for myself what the hell was going on? It was maddening.

Arolynn's voice called out for the first time since things had taken their beguiling turn.

"OK, Matthew! Sorry!"

"OK!" Bill echoed. "Let me move the car now."

Coming back up for air, Arolynn reappeared in my mirror. She then began walking up the driveway, as though nothing out of the ordinary had happened. Bill got back into their car and drove it a short distance to the cul-de-sac at the end of the street. At long last, I was able to back our rental out of the driveway, let Bill pull into the garage, and follow him into the driveway again, the long-awaited game of musical cars.

Everyone was filing into the house as I got out of the rental. None of them showed any inclination to volunteer what had transpired behind the car.

Just as Liz was about to step inside, I tugged on her arm.

"What happened!" I demanded, dying to know.

"Um, well," Liz began, her face again contorting into a laugh. "Arolynn just really had to go!"

"Had to go? What do you mean?"

The only thing that came to mind was that Arolynn had needed to pee. But that didn't make any sense. Not at the end of her driveway, nothing shielding her from neighbors who might drive by or peer out their windows in response to the commotion. Not when she was mere steps from her own front door, the bathroom just on the other side of it.

"She had to go!" Liz insisted through her laughter, as though that should have been enough for me to get it. "When she got up to get out of the car, she realized that she had to go so bad, she couldn't even make it to the house."

"You mean she went on the street?"

"Yes, she couldn't wait! That's why Bill couldn't move the car—she was peeing right there, right next to it!"

"And, oh my god," Arolynn began, as Liz and I made our way into the kitchen. "Once it started coming, it would not stop! It just kept coming and coming! It was like a lake!"

Now I was the one who was laughing. I could scarcely imagine having to pee so badly that I'd be forced to do so mere steps away from my own bathroom.

"Well, honey, when you get to be my age, you don't always have a choice."

"Like that time on BART!" Bill chimed in as he joined us, their little pooch following at his feet. A longhaired black lapdog, his ears were so big they got wet every time he drank from his bowl.

"Oh god!" Arolynn exclaimed, throwing her hands on top of her head. "That's one we'll never forget!"

"What happened?" I asked.

"Well, we were coming back from the City—I don't remember what we'd been doing, do you, honey?"

"A show?" Bill proposed, unsure.

"Yeah, maybe it was a show. Anyway, I went to the bathroom before we left, but it didn't matter. The ride home was too long."

"So, then she looks at me and she says, 'Honey, I'm sorry,' with a huge grin on her face. And when I ask her what she's sorry about, she just responds 'I couldn't wait.'"

"Well, I couldn't!" Arolynn bellowed.

"It took me a second, and then I thought, 'No. She didn't just—'"

"But I did! I wet myself on the train! Sitting there in my seat!"

"No way!" Liz and I cried in unison.

"Oh yes," Arolynn insisted. "Something to look forward to. You guys just wait."

Liz and I were leaving the next morning. We had breakfast. We packed our bags. We headed outside to load up the car.

"See, Matthew, I wasn't exaggerating," Arolynn observed behind me.

"About what?" I asked, turning toward her.

"There," she said, pointing to the road, another huge grin on her face.

"Oh my god," laughed Liz, before I had a chance to say anything.

"You really did pee out a lake!" I exclaimed in disbelief.

"And it's still there!" Liz cried.

In truth, Arolynn's puddle of pee had evaporated in the hot desert morning. Like an oil leak under an old car, it had nevertheless stained the road. I wouldn't have thought it possible. All I could figure was that her urine was so highly acidic, it had chemically reacted with the minerals in the pavement. About a foot wide where I presumed she had been standing, the discolored patch extended a full three feet, getting progressively narrower.

Arolynn hadn't been exaggerating. Her insistence that she had no chance of making it into the house before the deluge was now entirely credible. Camels wandering remote reaches of the Sahara probably carried less water than what she had expelled the night before.

"Stand next to it, so I can get a picture," I insisted. Arolynn graciously obliged. Her head held high, a cloudless blue sky as backdrop, she looked proud of her nearly superhuman feat.

Before we hit the road, I went to the bathroom.

I made sure Liz did the same.

11 MY LOST SOLE

I am not a luxury traveler.

You'll rarely hear me raving about the amazing place I stayed or the incredible service I got or the joys of having someone clean up after me day after day. Just as often as not, I find myself in places I couldn't possibly recommend in good conscience to my more discerning friends.

Or just about anyone else.

My little refuge high in the Barcelona sky was one such place. Even calling it a studio was a bit of a euphemism. For my needs, however, it could not have been more perfect.

The tiny room was just large enough for a full-size futon. There wasn't space for any other furniture, apart from a wall-mounted table that folded up when not in use. A couple of feet from the futon was a fireplace covered in smooth whitewash. Its mantle proudly displayed a photo of '80s Italian porn star and politician, Cicciolina, whose other claim to fame was being ex-wife to Jeff Koons. He was the renowned artist responsible for immortalizing Michael Jackson and his beloved chimp Bubbles in a giant porcelain sculpture. I recalled the privilege of having seen that incomparable work in person, a quasi-religious experience that had forever changed my appreciation of the evocative power of art. I couldn't help but wonder what had become of Bubbles.

To the left of the fireplace was the kitchen; or, rather, a hotplate and a sink.

And a toilet.

European kitchens often have washing machines. I'd never seen one with a toilet. Keeping an open mind, however, I immediately saw the advantages. In Copenhagen, I could relieve myself while showering. Here, I could snack. If I wanted to, in fact, there was nothing to stop me from having a full meal—the mini-fridge was a mere arm's length from the front of the commode. Scarcely moving a muscle, I could complete the entire digestive cycle, input in, input out, for days at a time. No need to go anywhere, as long as the refrigerator was stocked. The implications for my productivity were staggering.

The shower was on the other side of the fireplace. Inaccessible when the little table was in use, its walls were covered in bright-blue tiles. As eye-catching as they were, the true extent of the shower's beauty and mystique could only be appreciated from the inside.

The shower, it turned out, had a secret. Rather than the wall that ordinarily would have been expected there, the left side concealed an opening to a hidden staircase. I had known beforehand that the studio had a roof deck; what I hadn't known was that it was accessed through a secret passage in the shower.

Having made the discovery, I had to make the climb. It was a precarious one. The staircase made an ascent so steep, its steps were almost like rungs of a ladder. They were both taller and shallower than normal stairs, necessitating some sort of support; but the staircase was so narrow, there was no room for handrails. I stabilized myself by putting my hands against the walls, vowing to never make the climb under any sort of influence.

The views inside the studio were impressive enough, an identical square window in each wall opening onto unobstructed views of the city. From the roof, the views were even better. The Mediterranean was in plain sight. The mountains that surrounded the city, too. Were I feeling sacrilegious, I could practically spit on the 14th-century gothic basilica next door. The ornate spires of the cathedral in the center weren't much further away. I was living in the top of my own tower in the Gothic Quarter, and—once I covered the windows with mosquito screen, which I was grateful to discover sold by length at a local hardware store—I could not have been happier.

That didn't mean that life in the sky was without its challenges. On the contrary, in order to ensure my month-long stay transpired without incident, there were a few things of which it was imperative I not lose sight.

First there was the big switch over the kitchen toilet. If I wanted to go to the bathroom or take a shower or wash dishes, I had to flip on the switch for half an hour each morning. The switch turned on a pump, which filled the storage tank on the roof with a day's supply of water. Forgetting to turn it on meant I ran out of water. Forgetting to turn it off meant the tank overflowed, sending water cascading down the drain and out to sea, for as long as the pump was left running.

Remembering to turn the pump on and off was important. Remembering there was no floor under the kitchen was a matter of life and death.

In yet another ingeniously economical use of space, the hot plate and sink comprising the kitchen were built into a platform that hovered over the staircase leading up from the door to the apartment. There was no floor. There was no railing. One wrong move while frying an egg or scrubbing a plate, and you found yourself in a free fall, spiraling toward the foot of the stairs a full (and unusually high) floor below. The fact that the studio shared no walls with any neighbors made it considerably more likely you'd be lying there on your own, a bruised and bloodied mass of broken bones, until your scheduled departure date—assuming, of course, you weren't already among the dearly departed long before then.

I never fell from my studio. My shoe, on the other hand,

did. And it fell a lot further than just one floor.

I had just returned from one of my epic nighttime strolls. Shuttered retailers, abandoned banks, and empty offices were upstaged by bars, restaurants, and ice cream shops, all of them aglow and abustle. At three stops along the way, I had contemplated architectural gems designed by Antoni Gaudí, before losing myself in the quaint alleys of Gràcia. Narrow streets and spacious plazas were alive with music and laughter, joyful cries and impassioned debates. The air smelled of fried food and fine wine, of light wisps of tobacco and dense clouds of hash, of sporadic belches from unsavory sewers.

Leaving Gràcia behind, I crossed over to the more formal, grandiose avenues of l'Eixample. It, too, was residential; but, in comparison to where I'd been shortly before, it felt impersonal. The buildings were large. They were proud, many done in a breathtaking Modernist style.

Another wide boulevard came and went, and once again I found myself wandering medieval alleyways. These were part of El Raval, a traditionally working-class neighborhood long since overtaken by more illicit forms of commerce. Ladies of the evening worked the night shift. Covert exchanges were executed with discreet sleight of hand. Police made frequent, conspicuous rounds.

I crossed las Ramblas, throwing myself into the tide of tourists crammed onto the long, narrow strip stretching from the Plaça de Catalunya down to the sea, the constricted aorta of Barcelona's overworked and aching heart. The cathedral came and went soon after, floodlights illuminating its façade, stained glass, and spires.

After gliding like a ghost through another familiar maze of alleys, of dark stone archways and shadows thrown by lamplights, of deranged gargoyles with watchful eyes and wooden doors large enough for fortresses, I found myself fishing in my pocket. It didn't take long. The key to my building was comically large, a cartoon key for a cartoon keyhole—so round I could almost stick my pinky into it. The lock was a relic from the past, today more an act-as-if deterrent than a genuine impediment. The door itself looked solid enough to withstand a battering ram; the lock would have been as easy to pick as a snotty schoolboy's nose.

Once inside, I started climbing. I still hadn't determined exactly how many floors were stacked between the ground-level entryway and my studio in the clouds. There were quarter flights and half flights; there were flights as tall as floors, but lacking any doors; there were doors in close proximity that opened onto the stairwell at differing levels, the variances too small to account for whole floors but too big to be easily explained. My studio even had its own little metal staircase up to the door and another still behind it, setting it that much further apart from the rest of the building.

Regardless of the exact number—six, seven, even eight—there were a lot of floors. And so tonight—just like every night—as I made the marathon climb, my heart beat in protest and my lungs pumped uncomfortably hard. It was August in Barcelona. It was sweltering, even after dark. The stuffy stairwell was still holding onto the heat of the day. The higher I went, the more the hot, humid air pressed on me from all sides, intent on squeezing from me every last drop of sweat. My insistence on skipping steps and not stopping until I got to my door also worked against me.

I unlocked the studio and climbed the very last flight, again debating with myself whether this one counted as another floor. It was long enough, after all.

At the top of the stairs, I threw off my shoes. My feet sweat enough under normal conditions. Walking for hours in heat and humidity as bad as a southern swamp in summer only makes it that much worse. My new shoes reeked. They had crossed a point of no return, like fruit that's begun to rot. The tiny studio wasn't big enough for the three of us. My shoes would have to spend the night under the stars.

Outside the window over my collapsible table, there was a

non-functional air-conditioning unit. On top of it was a small shelf where a few small cacti reveled in the summer sun. I opened the window, and put one of my shoes on the shelf.

No sooner had I let it go, than the shoe was gone.

A resounding thud followed. The painful sound echoed off the buildings enclosing the courtyard behind my tower.

I stuck my head out the window to see what had happened.

The shelf wasn't flush with the outside wall. There was a gap of a few inches, not visible from inside the studio. My shoe had slipped right through that gap, plummeting a few stories below onto someone's roof. Except it wasn't really a roof. From what I could tell in the dark, it appeared to be some sort of plexiglass cover over the stairwell in an adjoining building. That explained why the shoe's fall had reverberated somewhat, as opposed to making the dull impact typical of a more solid surface.

I pulled myself back inside, out of an instinctive sense of self-preservation. I was sweating again. My heart raced. I held my breath.

The property managers had made it implicitly understood I wasn't supposed to be there (a minor detail they had waited to share until after I'd paid in full and flown halfway around the world). Barcelona was experiencing a crackdown on illegal vacation units; I assumed my studio was one of them. As long as I maintained a low profile, there was no problem. But what if I dropped a small bomb on my neighbors? In the middle of the night? Would that constitute a problem? The impact had been really loud. It was the kind of sound that suggests the need to check for damage, like the fateful crunch when two cars back into one another. I had just put an abrupt end to the impeccable discretion I'd shown thus far. What would happen now?

Creeping back to the window, I peered over the edge. The last time I'd been in a similar situation was many years before in Istanbul, when I had accidentally dropped a gallon-sized glass jug out my window. It fell four stories, landed on top of a car, and shattered. Everywhere. When I looked down to assess the damage, a man was glaring up at me. Thank god the jug hadn't landed on him. But what if he called the police? And what about the car owner? What if he was one of those macho youngsters who consider their vehicles an extension of themselves? What would he do when he came back?

I couldn't tell from so high up whether the vehicle was damaged, yet I was mortified to go down and check. My mind had flooded with worst-case scenarios and *Midnight Express* flashbacks. I didn't want to lose my tongue.

Returning to my current dilemma, I scanned the nearby buildings, the pit in my stomach getting bigger by the moment. One light after another, were angry neighbors about to wake up? Would they soon be scaling my tower, ripping through the mosquito screen I'd so carefully installed with thumbtacks and duct tape, and coming at me from all sides? Were they going to lay siege to my dwelling from below, starving me into submission (which wouldn't take long, given the size of the mini-fridge)? Perhaps the authorities were already making their way upstairs—taking so long only because one of them had passed out halfway up? Should I be expecting a demanding knock at my door, the Guardia Civil asking for my papers, only to then escort me—my head lowered in shame, my hands in shackles, an enraged mob shouting insults at me in *català*, the regional language—to the *comisaría*? What had I done to deserve this? How had my life spun so quickly out of control?

I waited.

Would I get the one free call, like at home?

I waited some more.

Would it be a problem that my call would have to be an overseas one? I didn't have any friends in Barcelona. I didn't have an international calling plan.

No lights came on. Neither projectiles nor shouts were hurled at my tower, nor were there any signs of bonfires being built at its base. I didn't hear footsteps at my door, let alone angry knocks or staticky walkie-talkies. Maybe the agents had been forced to turn around. Maybe their light-headed comrade required medical attention.

I waited a few more moments. Still nothing.

I retreated inside and opened a bottle of wine.

I was grateful to have been spared the wrath of my neighbors, never mind a visit from the authorities, the night before. Still, the next morning there was a problem.

I needed my shoe.

I went up to the roof deck to assess the situation.

I spotted my fallen footwear immediately, a few stories below. It looked tragically out of place, like a precious possession accidentally discarded with the trash. It looked lonely, too, separated as it was from its better half. The more I contemplated it, however, the clearer it became: rescuing my shoe was going to be difficult. Although I could see it, I didn't know where it was. Not exactly.

The Gothic Quarter was a hodgepodge of densely crowded edifices built practically one on top of the other over hundreds of years. Trying to judge from overhead on which building my shoe had landed was difficult at best. I couldn't even tell for sure if the rooftop in question corresponded to a building that opened onto an alley. It looked more like it was set back from the street. Consequently, I had no way of knowing where to inquire about my shoe—there were too many facades crammed too closely together in the crowded alleyways. And, again, it seemed unlikely that the building where my shoe had fallen was even one of them.

I gave it more thought, looking despondently below. I was going to have to let the shoe go. In reality, after all, it had slipped through my fingers the night before. So close, yet so far away. I went round and round a few more times, finally resigning myself to the sorry truth.

I would have to buy a new pair of shoes.

The more I thought about it in the hours that followed, the less it felt right. I had bought the shoes specifically for my travels. Since I knew I'd be doing a lot of walking, I had spent real money on them—they weren't cheap. And I liked them. A lot. Green and blue, with lots of support, they were comfortable and stylish, both functional and fashionable. I could wear them with shorts during the day; they were nice enough for those rare occasions when I needed to get relatively dressed up. They were what I needed. They were what I wanted. Why should I have to shop for another pair, when I already had the perfect one?

Other than the fact that half the pair was lying on a roof three stories below.

There had to be a way.

Once I opened myself to the possibility, I couldn't stop thinking about it. The challenge took on a life of its own. Proving to myself that I could overcome the impossible came to feel almost as important as saving my lost sole.

Soon I was circling down the staircase. Once outside, I made a beeline for a sporting goods store. I knew it from a previous trip.

Although I was going to a sporting goods store, what I needed had nothing to do with traditional sports. Ignoring tennis rackets and soccer balls and swim goggles, I asked to be pointed to the outdoors section; specifically, to the fishing gear. Once there, I grabbed some line, a metal sinker, and a large three-pronged hook. It was frightening, sharp like a raptor's talons. That was the idea. My hope was that the hook would soon be swooping down from the sky, snatching up my shoe like an eagle seizing its prey.

Back at the apartment, I rushed through the shower and up to the roof. I looked down. In my absence, neither seagulls nor sewer rats had made off with my shoe. There was still time.

I attached the sinker and hook to the end of the fishing line. I then approached the edge of the terrace, scanning the neighboring buildings. A fit young man was sunning on his third-story patio across the courtyard. Otherwise, the coast appeared clear—although I couldn't be sure, since the angle of the sunlight prevented me from seeing into all the windows. Having been spared the night before any unpleasant interactions with the authorities, I didn't want to rouse suspicions now.

I sent the hook and sinker sailing.

My first attempt landed way off the mark. I'd need a few warm-up tosses before I got a sense for my unusual instrument, for its weight, its awkward shape, and how the line affected the arc of its fall.

No less of a consideration was the edge of the terrace. The wall wasn't very high. Throwing the hook and sinker required the intense concentration of a beanbag toss, compromising my sense of where I was in relation to the wall. If I wasn't careful, I'd end up like the shoe, stories below.

I threw the hook and sinker again. Several times. It didn't take long before I had an audience. The young sun worshipper sat up in his lounge chair, lowering his shades to get a better look. A few people inside the nearby buildings gathered at the windows. As if the situation weren't already challenging enough, I now had to deal with performance anxiety. My fear of having to explain myself to the police also returned.

The shoe was too far from the wall. After multiple failed attempts, I threw in the towel. Sports requiring good aim, like darts or horseshoes, had never been my forte. The bright sun, an unpredictable sea breeze, and prying eyes had further sabotaged my efforts.

I retreated indoors for a nap.

When I woke up a while later, a variation to my technique came to me in a flash of inspiration. I went back upstairs. The sun wasn't as strong. There was scarcely a breeze. No one was watching.

Now was my chance.

I removed the sinker, leaving just the hook on the end of the line. I then clearly visualized the hook sailing through the air and landing in the perfect spot, just beyond my shoe.

I tossed.

I missed.

As I drew the line back in, I took a deep breath. Again, I visualized the hook falling in just the right place.

I tossed.

The hook sailed through the air, landing a couple of feet beyond my shoe.

My heart jumped. Ever so carefully—trying to stay calm—I pulled on the line. The three-pronged metal claw scooted across the plexiglass surface, skipping slightly as it met with occasional resistance. But then, with one fateful bounce, one of the hooks pierced the side of the shoe, like a trident spearing a fish. I felt a burst of elation.

The ordeal wasn't over, however. I still had to drag the shoe over to and up the wall.

Unlike doing battle with a deep-sea catch, reeling in my shoe was not an exercise in brute force. Neither was it about speed. I had no idea how securely the hook was stuck into the shoe. For all I knew, the slightest miscalculation, and I'd be back at square one.

Slowly but surely, I tightened the line until it was taut. I then began dragging the shoe toward the wall. The shoe resisted. It had a cumbersome form, not made for sliding. The sole was rubber, expressly designed for gripping surfaces. All the same, the plexiglass was both flat and smooth enough to compensate for anything limiting the shoe's movement. Soon the shoe was at the wall.

I felt encouraged. I was even more hopeful. But, again, how securely had the hook lodged itself into the shoe? Enough to defy gravity? Enough to support the shoe's weight as it took to the air? Would the hook's hold withstand additional pressure as the shoe repeatedly bounced off the side of the building on its way up? For three full stories?

I took another deep breath and began reeling in the line.

The shoe weighed more than I thought. But it didn't bounce off the wall as much as I had expected. After it had climbed about a floor, I was convinced the hook was lodged deeply enough to hold the shoe for the duration. Still, I feared becoming overconfident, jeopardizing the entire endeavor. I redoubled my focus, forcing myself to be that much more deliberate; to stay in control, so I didn't lose it.

Before long the shoe was nearly within reach. I longed to meet it halfway, to welcome it back to the rooftop like a mother opening her loving arms to her long-lost child. Instead, I stayed on my side of the wall, continuing to methodically pull the fishing line. I would not allow myself to get overeager. I'd never be able to live with myself if I lost the shoe now.

Finally, as if it were the most natural thing in the world, as though it had been a foregone conclusion since its plummet the night before, my free-fallen footwear vaulted over the terrace wall like a high jumper over a bar.

Reunited, and it felt so good.

I rushed the shoe downstairs for what was sure to be an even more emotional reunion.

12 A TURKISH BATH IN MOROCCO

During the entire year I lived in Istanbul, I never made it to a hammam. Given that I'm ordinarily keen on taking full advantage of the cultural experiences that are unique to—or, especially in this case, even emblematic of—the places I visit, I'd never been able to forgive myself for the oversight.

Just like the old Turkish toilets, those glorified holes in the ground over which countless legions of squatters have played a bizarre sort of scatological target practice, Turkish baths have a long history all their own. Over time they became fixtures not only in their homeland but far beyond its borders, particularly throughout the Arab world.

Consequently, it came as little surprise when, at an otherwise relatively uninspired stop in my travels, I discovered a hammam not far from my hotel. I didn't give it a second thought. The time had come to right a horrible wrong, one that had weighed on my conscience for far, far too long.

I was going to a Turkish bath in Morocco.

I asked the two women at the hotel front desk for the lowdown. I already knew that whereas in Turkey a towel wrapped around the waist is customary, in Morocco men are required to wear bathing suits. I wondered what else I needed to know.

Both women seemed delighted I had not only shown an interest in but was actually about to partake of one of their most hallowed traditions. Taking me under their wings as if temporarily adopting a son, they briefed me on the *dos* and *don'ts*. They also provided me with flip-flops and a colorful plastic pail. Feeling like a child headed for a day at the beach, rather than a grown man seeking a deeper connection to a people and place though an ancient ritual, I set off to make peace with my past and expand my cultural horizons.

Easily finding my way to the hammam, I opened the door and stepped inside. A subdued peace and quiet of the sort usually reserved for places of worship reigned over a small lobby. A dimly lit, self-contained world, it seemed somehow impervious to the blinding midday sun and the cacophony of the city outside.

A staircase climbed upwards to my left, coming to an abrupt halt at a closed door. Benches lined the wall opposite me as well as the one to my right, the reception area also serving as changing room, oddly enough. Under each bench were small cubby holes with doors. Over the benches were narrow, cloudy windows more effective at holding the daylight at bay than allowing it inside.

Before beginning the tragic descent into its present state of neglect, the building had seen much better days, signs of its faded glory discernible everywhere I looked. The ceiling that had once soared majestically overhead must have been begging for a new coat of paint for years, blemished by peeling patches so deep they exposed bone-white plaster. The carpets were threadbare, their worn fibers like veins stripped of their flesh, and the once elegant stairway had lost its luster, cluttered by haphazard piles of boxes and all sorts of forgotten junk.

On the other side of the room, an old man sat behind a simple desk. He saw me enter, but neither said a word nor moved a muscle. I couldn't help but wonder if he hadn't been there as long as the hammam itself, having become an inseparable part of it, a lover who'd be lost without it. I walked over and inquired how much it would cost to use the baths.

"*Massage?*" he asked.

I hadn't expected the question, but I didn't have to think twice about the answer. I'd been traveling for almost a week, burdened by a large backpack and sitting on cramped buses for hours at a time, my back a contorted mass of knots. A massage was exactly what my sore and aching body needed.

"*Oui*," I replied.

I paid the man and found a place on one of the benches. Taking off my clothes, I put on my bathing suit, a little self-conscious about doing so in plain sight of the stoic set of eyes observing me such a short distance away. It wasn't until I went to put my belongings in a cubby hole that I noticed there weren't any locks on the doors. The cubbies were little more than cupboards, as opposed to full-fledged lockers. I hesitated, once again turning to the man, who had anticipated my question and gestured dismissively. He was sitting right there, and no one else was around. Besides, I had left my passport and other valuables at the hotel. I didn't have anything to worry about.

Once I was ready, the man ushered me through a door to his right, into a room that might have been unremarkable, had it not contrasted so dramatically with the reception area. It was as if I'd unknowingly made the descent to a lower level of the edifice, a tenebrous netherworld where the walls, floor, and ceiling were all made of the same gray stone. A heavy vapor hung on the air and light was scarce, as though unwelcome there.

I was now alone, uneasy like someone arriving at a haunted house in the middle of nowhere only to watch the door close behind them. In this case, however, I was standing in the darkness, wearing a bathing suit and flip-flops and holding a silly plastic pail I could have been using to build sand castles. Everything seemed a little off.

It wasn't long before an enormous older man emerged out of nowhere. He was, to be sure, an astonishing sight: a fleshy giant with the palest of skin, the thinnest of hair, and the dimmest and dullest of expressions. Everything about him suggested that if he had ever seen the light of day, he had no recollection of it.

Just like me, he carried a bucket, which he dipped into a large basin of steaming water on the other side of the room. Unlike me, he wore an obscenely small, dingy pair of underwear that clung precariously to his sweaty buttocks and groin. Saturated to lurid transparency, it came nowhere close to containing the fleshy undulations of his enormous body. In spite of myself, I stared like the witness to a car wreck, snapped out of my stupor only when he turned and looked my way, our eyes locking.

Diverting my gaze, I wondered where my masseur was. Maybe I was being impatient, but it seemed he was taking an unreasonably long time to come find me. He was probably just finishing up with another customer, I told myself, trying to relax. For all I knew, he was still preparing the room, putting clean sheets on the massage table or making sure he had everything else in order before our session.

Often we discover that what we're looking for is right under our noses.

Although the corpulent behemoth now lumbering toward me wouldn't have come even close to fitting under my nose—which scarcely reached beyond his hairy navel—it turned out that he was, nonetheless, exactly what I had been looking for.

"*Massage?*" he asked, with what seemed like a mischievous grin. I wondered why he suddenly looked so happy, overwhelmed by the uneasy feeling I was about to become the butt of a very bad joke.

"Ah, yes ..." I hesitated, my eyes darting in all directions in hopes of finding a quick way out. I didn't have the guts to tell him that putting myself at the mercy of a nearly naked ogre three times my size made me a little uncomfortable. Instead, though kicking and screaming inside, outside I offered no resistance, obediently following my captor deeper into the darkness.

While it didn't even come close to the descriptions I had heard of beautiful old marble-covered Turkish hammams, the main chamber wasn't completely devoid of charm. The walls and floor were identical to those in the previous room and, as such, relatively plain; but, the ceiling took the form of an elegant dome perforated by tiny circular windows. Through each of their translucent panes, a precise beam pierced the steamy obscurity, affording the naked eye just enough light to get a sense of the surroundings.

The man gestured for me to sit down on a stone bench and rinse myself with the hot water from the basin. I did so, after which he went to get more. Looking around, I noticed there were only two other men in the hammam, engaged in hushed conversation on the far side of the room. I would have preferred there be a few more people, but at least I was no longer alone.

When the man returned with the water, he seemed to be gesturing for me to get onto the floor. I knew that couldn't be right, but I had no way of asking him to clarify, since my attempts—first in French, then in Spanish, and finally in English—were all met with silence.

Not interested in dillydallying, the masseur took me by the hand, raising it so I'd stand up. Once I had, he again pointed to the floor, more commandingly this time.

Not only could it be right, but it was.

He wanted me on my knees.

Despite my hesitance, I reluctantly obeyed, reminding myself he was the one who knew how this was all supposed to work, not I. I just had to go with it. Or, to be more precise, I just had to kneel before him, not actually going anywhere at all.

The giant wasted no time dousing my upper body yet again, only to then unleash a full-on assault with a soapy wet rag. For the first time since entering the hammam, I began to relax. The water was warm and it felt good, as did having someone attentively scrub my body. The deep cleaning went well beyond what I could do on my own, removing layers of all sorts of grime I hadn't even realized was there. I felt something like I feel when sitting in a barber's chair, the soothing touch on my scalp always lulling me into a state of utter relaxation, if not gentle slumber.

No sooner had he finished scouring my upper body and arms, than I had the surreal impression the man was making another, even more bizarre request. Rather than merely kneel on the floor, he seemed to be asking me to lie down on it.

I'm not even remotely a germophobe. Unless you're about to perform surgery, I think hand sanitizer is ridiculous, yet another product cleverly designed and ingeniously marketed to keep consumers in a constant state of paranoia. I'll drink from friends' cups, I never bother to put antiseptic on cuts, and I am an unapologetic, lifelong adherent to the three-second rule, rarely having any issues with picking up food that's fallen to the floor and putting it into my mouth without the slightest hesitation.

But this wasn't just any floor.

This was a grimy, slimy floor. The same floor on which my maternal hotel guardians had insisted I wear flip-flops, an absolute hygienic necessity, protection against an untold number of unimaginable health hazards lying on the damp stone like predators in wait. A floor rising up from which I was almost certain I could hear the mating calls and battle cries of countless unknown strains of bacteria, fungi that were sure to colonize each and every crevice of my body, and viruses that science had yet to develop any means of combating. All of them were glaring up at me like lions pacing about their dens, greedily anticipating how they would ravage their next meal when it fell from the sky.

Kowtowing to be at the right level for the masseur to do his job was one thing; pressing my entire body against the mysterious muck on the floor was another altogether.

It didn't matter.

Before I could protest—something I probably wouldn't have done anyway, for reasons I've already explained—the giant had taken me by the shoulders and pushed me toward the floor. By no means was he violent, but neither did he leave any doubt as to what I was supposed to do.

Lying on my back, my body was soon as riddled with

anxiety as the ceiling was with its tiny holes. I could no longer see the masseur, so I had no idea what he was doing—or going to do—and I couldn't stop thinking about the fact I was lying in filth. When my own dead skin, clumps of hair, and unseen microbes had tumbled to the floor, no one had run out from behind a curtain to mop it all up. Who else's dirt, germs, and bodily fluids had welcomed mine as they joined them in a debaucherous orgy? On second thought, never mind. I didn't want to know. After all, it was now all over my back, which, whether merely due to the power of suggestion or because of infectious outbreaks now underway, had begun to itch.

It was then that the giant reappeared, coming between me and the constellation of lights overhead like the moon eclipsing not only the sun but all the stars. Despite the stifling heat, his dark shadow gave me a foreboding chill. For the first time it occurred to me that if he decided to harm me in any way, there wasn't a thing I could do about it—something I struggled with even more as he proceeded to climb all over my body.

Besides having all three-hundred-plus of his fleshy pounds ready to crush me at any moment, should he slip on the wet stone or his arms buckle under his own weight, what was to come involved not only scalding water, but a new rag that may as well have been made of steel wool.

News the next phase was underway shot from one end of my nervous system to the other like a summer wildfire backed by strong winds. Between the blistering temperature of the water and the stinging fibers of the rag, I wasn't sure what hurt more. While I gave it some thought, the giant made his way up my body, beginning with my legs, deferentially bypassing the family jewels, and proceeding up my torso. Once he got to my shoulders, he extended each of my arms as if he were also about to crucify me. Truth be told, it probably would have felt better than what followed.

As though letting out a lifetime of anger to which he'd never been able to give voice, the giant took it up a notch. His massive gut mere inches from my face, he scrubbed my helpless body with a relentless fury. I closed my eyes and shut my mouth as a salty shower of sweat rained down on me, holding my breath. It was agonizing, and I wasn't sure it was ever going to end.

Just as I was about to reach my breaking point, it finally did.

Or so I thought.

While I was still writhing in pain, breathless like a fish flopping around on the bow of a boat, my so-called masseur jumped into a bizarre practice that would have been completely foreign to any massage therapist I've ever known. To a pastry chef, on the other hand, the technique would have been all too familiar.

Like dough that needed to be molded into a perfect pie crust, he began pinching both sides of my torso from top to bottom.

Hard.

It was excruciating—the steel wool paling in comparison. I couldn't help but wonder if there'd be any skin left on my body when the sadistic ritual was finally over.

As I was about to let out a desperate cry that would require no translation, the giant finished putting the final touches on what was essentially the icing on the cake. Successfully making the Herculean effort to stand back up, he then retreated to someplace deep in the hammam's secret underworld, leaving me flinching on the floor like a bug that's been smashed but isn't quite dead. Staring up at the pretty beams of light, I wondered why they were spinning.

I have no idea how long I lay there. I was stunned, struggling with exactly what part of the ordeal could have possibly been considered the "massage." When it finally came time to peel myself from the floor, I felt like an egg stuck to a dirty frying pan—I practically needed someone to scrape me off it. Given that my entire body felt so raw, I also couldn't help but wonder if the giant hadn't drawn blood, which almost seemed to have been his goal.

Once I succeeded in propping myself up, I sat in the steam for a short while longer, my senses slowly returning to me. Repeatedly reliving the absurd experience in an attempt to make sense of it, I eventually conceded there was no point and decided to head back to the hotel.

No sooner did I get to my room, than I stood in the mirror and took off my shirt.

I hadn't been imagining things.

In the reflection of my torso I beheld four butchered patches of flesh where blood had seeped to the surface. Some of it had already scabbed, while other areas were still speckled with bright-red drops of freshly oxygenated blood.

The giant had indeed been so rough he had made me bleed. If lying on the floor of the hammam was potentially risky, what could be the ramifications of doing so with open wounds? I prayed the water had been hot enough to kill any infectious agents and hoped for the best, hand sanitizer no longer seeming like such a bad idea after all.

13 STRANGERS IN THE NIGHT

Christine and I met in San Francisco, on a corporate gig where we were both contracting.

When, not long after, we were tasked with working on a project together, we went for coffee. As Christine gave me an overview of what the project entailed, its scope and assumptions and risks and other essential but mind-numbing facts and figures, I tried to take her seriously. I tried really hard. But an overwhelming feeling in my gut would not be ignored: it was all a charade. The reason Christine and I had met was not about collaborating on the advancement of the financial services industry, however lofty its goals.

I burst into uncontrollable laughter.

Christine stopped mid-sentence, her eyes cartoon-wide, dramatically out of proportion with her otherwise fine facial features. Blonde and blue-eyed, attractive and athletic, a Stanford grad and former corporate lawyer, her impeccable professionalism had been obliterated by my unexpected outburst, which could not have been more inappropriate.

Soon we were both laughing so hard neither of us could see through our tears.

We've been friends ever since.

Besides working jobs neither of us actually wanted to be doing, Christine and I had a lot in common. We had a similar sense of humor. We both loved the outdoors, and spent lots of time on the trails. We were both Francophiles, and had spent extended periods in France. It wasn't long before we were imagining how great it would be to go to France together. Soon we were planning a trip, something made that much easier by a fortuitous event a couple of months earlier.

Christine's corporate gig was just a means to end, a way to refill the coffers after taking a few years off when she ended her career as an attorney. As for what she really wanted to do, she was still trying to figure that out.

One night she went to a lecture. The speaker was one of the most powerful men in the world at the time. Given his prominent role in international affairs—an area in which Christine already had experience and was exploring new possibilities—she decided to hang around after the talk to ask him a few questions.

What he decided to do was ask her out.

She accepted.

Thus began one of those painfully ambiguous relationships where one person knows exactly what they want, but the other's not quite so sure. There was wining and dining. There was transcontinental texting. There were overseas rendezvous.

There was an apartment in Paris.

Christine didn't have to ask twice. We were welcome to use her friend's place, although he would be in Switzerland during our stay.

The apartment was all ours.

It wasn't just any apartment. Before the wall had been knocked out, in fact, there had been two separate units, each in a different building. A quarter flight of stairs now joined them, two bedrooms and a bath on one side, the living room and kitchen on the other, slightly more elevated, level.

Medieval wood beams held up the ceilings. The rooms were decorated with original works of art. The hardwood floors were adorned with fine silk rugs. The kitchen and bath were redone with high-end tile, fixtures, and appliances. Everything was top-notch.

All that was fine and good; but, in real estate, one thing matters three times more than anything else: location, location, location. Lest the apartment fail to live up to its own high standards, that proved to be its coup de grace: it was located kitty-corner to the Centre Pompidou; in other words, it was in the very heart of the City of Lights, on one of its most prestigious squares.

It was perfect, which only made the bathroom incident several days after our arrival that much more absurd.

Sitting down on the toilet to take care of business, I was exhausted. I hadn't gotten much sleep the night before. Around two or three in the morning, I'd been awakened by unfamiliar voices. Lying in bed half-conscious, at first it seemed strange. When I realized the voices were coming from inside the apartment, it became alarming.

All the more so when a young man barged into my room.

"*Pardon! Désolé!*" he apologized, closing the door as quickly as he had burst it open.

The sun may have been down, but the intruder had just scared the living daylights out of me. My heart was racing.

Who was he? What was he doing in the apartment? And why had he stormed into my bedroom? At least he hadn't slit my throat.

My initial shock giving way to anger, I jumped out of bed, threw on some pants, and stormed up the stairs to the living room. I was surprised by what I found. The room was lit by candlelight. It was serene, almost romantic, even. There were voices, but they were hushed.

I was still more surprised to find Christine sitting on the floor with not one, not two, but three handsome thirty-something-year-old men. She and I had each done our own thing the night before. I had met up with an old friend; she had gone out by herself. As I now discovered, that did not mean she had spent the evening alone.

And her evening wasn't over.

Already shaken from the intruder bursting into my bedroom, now I was even more upset. Three men? Back to the apartment her lovesick—and still hopeful—suitor had been kind enough to let her use? An apartment full of his fine art and expensive furnishings, his personal belongings? No less of an issue was her failure to show me the courtesy of any sort of heads-up. If she had brought home some guy for a romantic tryst, that would have been one thing; three of them felt reckless, if not potentially dangerous. I was livid.

I was also a gracious host.

One-by-one, Christine introduced me to her new friends, Jean, Jacques, and Jean-Jacques. Caught off guard yet again, I played along, biting down hard on my tongue and swallowing my anger. When one of the men discretely buttoned his pants, I pretended not to notice.

After shaking hands I regretted having touched, I returned to my room, still shaking with anger. I didn't sleep the rest of the night. I was too worked up.

The next morning, I left before Christine crawled out of her room. After her long night, she'd be getting up late. And for all I knew, she had an entire brood in her love nest. If so, I had no desire to be forced into more small talk with strangers. I spent the day migrating from café to café and roaming the streets.

The apartment was empty when I returned from my wanderings, my legs exhausted and my feet aching. The first thing I saw when I opened the door was a note on the kitchen table. Christine had left a lengthy apology for her poor judgment and lack of consideration. No one had spent the night.

In the meantime, fresh air, sunshine, and lots of walking had bolstered my mood. It had also given me perspective on my nightmare the night before, the one in which a stranger had stumbled into my room, followed by own stumbling into a scene with all the makings of an orgy. If I hadn't been awakened the way I had, I wouldn't have been so upset. And, although I still didn't appreciate Christine bringing home three guys, I could have given her the benefit of the doubt regarding their character.

Sitting in the bathroom now, my digestive system's obstinance an all-too-familiar rebuttal to my Parisian diet of pastries, bread and cheese, and chocolate, my eyes fell upon a candle. Christine had since come home, and must have lit the candle when she'd been in the restroom a little while before me. As the flame flickered, I was reminded of an incident years earlier. It hadn't taken place in Paris, but it did involve a *Parisienne*.

My friend Sophie had just arrived from France, and we were relaxing over a couple of glasses of wine. The apartment was lit by the soft glow of candlelight. One glass down, Sophie excused herself to go to the bathroom. Since I lived in a small studio, I turned up the music to give her some privacy. Sophie had long struggled with debilitating flatulence, and—as I myself knew all too well—prolonged periods in pressurized cabins only made it that much worse.

The toilet flushed and Sophie screamed. As I jumped to my feet to rush to her aid, she jumped out of the bathroom, enveloped in a noxious odor. Despite some memorable movements of my own, I'd never smelled anything like it. Not fried onions. Not roasted garlic. Even when I was a carnivore, not the lowest quality of beef. Nothing I'd ever eaten had resulted in such an unbearable stench. It was like a rancid sort of death.

"My hair caught on fire!" she exclaimed, still in a panic.

Sophie's hair was—or had been—a couple of inches shy of shoulder length. For whatever reason, she had bent down at the sink. Her hair had fallen into a candle burning next to it.

That explained the sickening smell. Burnt hair.

"How'd you put it out?" I asked, still alarmed, looking her up and down, as though fearing a spark might reignite, turning her into a fireball.

"With my hands!" she replied. "I didn't even think about it. When I looked in the mirror and saw the flames, I just grabbed at them."

I understood her reaction. In high-school chemistry class, my sweater sleeve had dangled for just a little too long over the transparent flame of a Bunsen burner. When my arm caught fire, my reflexive response—like Sophie's moments before—had been to snuff out the flames with my bare hand. Surprisingly, it proved no worse for the wear. I couldn't help but think I'd be a natural at fire walking.

As for Sophie's hair, it had always been a tangled, split-ended disaster. I'd seen more orderly rat's nests. Perhaps burning some of it off was for the best, like scorching a field so it can lay fallow, setting the stage for a period of renewal. I pondered a delicate way of suggesting Sophie ride the momentum and take it one step further, shaving her head and making a fresh start. If she was ashamed of having set herself on fire, she could just say she'd caught a nasty case of lice.

My business finally finished, my buttocks so fast asleep they'd taken on a bluish hue, I snapped out of my rumination and reached for the toilet paper. As I did, at eye level, on the countertop mere inches from my face, I saw something I couldn't immediately place.

It was white. And red, darker and thicker in some spots than others. It was papery, but fuzzy, too. Long and narrow, it looked like some sort of waste—but it wasn't anything I'd ever seen before. Even if I had, it wouldn't have been from the close proximity from which I observed it now. It was in my face.

I gagged.

Having grown up in a household with three women, I should have known. But, for whatever reason, until now, I'd never seen one before. Not a used one, that is.

Christine was celebrating her monthly communion with the Divine Feminine. Had she intentionally left me an invitation to the party?

Aghast, I looked away. Needing to confirm what I'd just seen, I looked back.

It was exactly what I thought it was.

I broke into hysterics.

"Christine!" I yelled, struggling to even say her name, given how hard I was laughing.

When she didn't respond, I hollered again.

"Christine!"

"What?" she replied, approaching the door. "Did you call me?"

"Yes!" I cried, now nearly sobbing.

"Why? What are you doing in there?"

"Did you forget something?"

"Forget something? What do you mean?"

She had no idea.

"What I mean is that I think you forgot something—and it's about three inches from my face!"

A pause followed, evidently not a pregnant one.

"Oh my god!" she gasped. "Oh. My. God. I am so, so sorry!"

Additional invocations and apologies followed.

And then, horror giving way to humor, Christine, too, lost it.

Laughter is the best medicine. Christine had already apologized for the night before, and I had accepted her apology. All the same, it was only now, Christine's used maxi pad in my face, that the air was really cleared.

14 A REAL SHORTAGE

California was not the first place I experienced a water shortage.

In fact, compared to what I lived on a daily basis in Istanbul, it's not even fair to say I "experienced" a water shortage in San Francisco. We knew there was a drought, so we tried to save water. I watered my garden less. I replaced plants that died with succulents. I stopped taking baths. Perhaps most important, if it was yellow, I let it mellow.

And yet water always rained down from the showerhead. Even when, the drought at its most severe, we were shocked day after day by pictures of reservoirs turned to deserts; of impossibly dry earth riddled with painful cracks, lifeless where, ordinarily, there would be glittering blue; water miraculously flowed from the tap.

Not so when I lived in Turkey.

I was just out of college. My stay in Istanbul had been made possible by the sale of my old Nissan Sentra hatchback. Given my intention to live in Turkey for at least a year, I couldn't survive on those proceeds—the sum total of my life savings—alone. Hence the teaching job I'd gotten when I arrived. It paid the local hourly rate. It wasn't some lucrative gig like those Japanese ones where young teachers are offered high-paying contracts with most of their expenses covered. I wasn't even certified to teach.

Given my limited resources, I had no illusions of living in luxury. But I did care about location—and I was eager to put an end to a string of temporary housing situations. So, when I heard about a room in the city center, I asked my Turkish friend, Neşe, to go with me to see it. An attractive, good-natured woman in her mid-twenties—a few years older than I was at the time—she managed the school where I was teaching.

The flat with the room was in the middle of everything. Taksim square, the de facto center of the city, its very heart, was a five-minute walk away. I'd never miss a single, teargas-filled protest. When the tanks rolled in—as indeed they would—I'd be one of the first to see them.

Istiklal Caddesi, Istanbul's main pedestrian street, was even closer. Cafés, bars, and restaurants. Cinemas, bookstores, and cultural centers. Little could I have known, but just steps from my apartment I'd soon be participating in a French *cercle littéraire* and even learning Kurdish dance. And taking guitar lessons. In Turkish. At the Kurdish association. Everything I could possibly need for both expanding my cultural horizons and finding myself a political prisoner would be right at my doorstep. The Turks and Kurds, after all, had long been engaged in a messy civil war in the country's southeast.

If I went the other direction, if I wanted to breathe comparatively fresh air and feel an invigorating sea breeze, if I wanted to watch oil tankers dwarfing everything they passed on their way to and from the Sea of Marmara, I could walk down the long, steep hill to the Bosphorus. I could even walk to work, if I wasn't in a hurry and felt up to a little exercise.

It was perfect.

A short, plump, animated landlady in her seventies welcomed us. Her flat was in a historic old building built by a pasha, a high-ranking Ottoman official. Or, so she said. Of course, it very well might have been true. But even if it was, the building's glory days had long since passed. No one of any means lived there now. It was to make ends meet that the landlady rented out three of her rooms.

She showed us the one that was available. There was nothing to it. A single bed with a lumpy mattress. Yellowing wallpaper with a forgettable floral pattern creeping up from the floor. Unusually high ceilings, and an unusually tall window overlooking the alley a few stories below. There was also a simple nightstand and an electric space heater—essential, since the apartment didn't have central heat, and it was the middle of winter.

After our quick look at the bedroom, the landlady, Ayten, escorted Neşe and me into the living room. Over little glasses of the ubiquitous Black Sea black tea—as much a part of Turkish culture as *döners* and kebabs—we got acquainted and discussed the apartment.

Things seemed to be going well until, out of the blue, Neşe frowned. The conversation was taking place in Turkish, which I hardly spoke.

"Metyu," Neşe began, turning to me.

There's no *th* sound in Turkish. Like so many English speakers hopelessly unable to roll their *r*s, the vast majority of Turks couldn't pronounce *th* if it meant a lifetime supply of Turkish delight. Consequently, for the year I lived in Istanbul, I ceased to be MATH-you. Instead, I became MATE-you.

"She is trying to ask a higher price," Neşe explained.

"Oh," I said. I should have been alarmed. Maybe even angered. I wasn't. Perhaps I was too overwhelmed by my sense of déjà vu. During a previous interview for a prospective roommate situation, the renter, a peculiar, unstable twenty-something, had doodled nonstop while we talked. When she looked away, I glanced at her paper. It was covered in dollar signs.

"She sees you are a foreigner," Neşe said, "so she thinks you have money."

"If I had money would I really want to rent a tiny room in a dilapidated old building with roommates I've never met? She knows I'm working for you, right? I mean, I'm grateful for the job and everything, but it's not like I'm doing it just for fun—I promise there's no trust fund."

"I know," Neşe laughed. "I will explain to her that you are not a rich American."

Neşe and Ayten had another brief exchange. We quickly settled on a price, somewhere between the original and the screw-the-foreigner one. I moved in (i.e., I showed up with my backpack) a couple of days later.

Neşe went with me again. When we got there, Ayten gave us another tour of the apartment, this one more like an orientation.

I was in for quite a surprise.

I hadn't noticed on my first visit, because I never would have known to look for them. Then, of course, there was the fact that they were camouflaged, under shelves and tables and strategically placed decorative fabrics. They blended perfectly into the surroundings, despite lining the halls and taking up space in the kitchen and making the bathroom that much more of a tight squeeze. They were everywhere there was any space for them.

Big plastic containers of water.

A key stopover on the old Silk Road, forever located at the infamous crossroads of Asia and Europe, even today Istanbul was known for drug smuggling, arms trafficking, and all sorts of other illicit activities. Was water now so scarce in this part of the world that it had become a precious commodity? Was Ayten some sort of water smuggler? Or, maybe instead, she was a new, climate-change-induced breed of hoarder, one with a deathly fear of going without water? Was Ayten an aqua-hoarder?

Almost.

"*Su yok! Su yok!*" she repeated, convinced that if she said it over and over, a little louder each time, until she was practically yelling, I'd eventually understand. It was her version of immersive language instruction. "*Su yok!*"

"Metyu, the water only comes sometimes," Neşe began, before being interrupted. Ayten had a few things to add. As I would learn soon enough, Ayten always had a few things to add.

"In a week, maybe only two days it is coming," Neşe continued. "So, Ayten *hanım* saves the water in the plastic ... uh, boxes, or what you want to call them."

"Really? Only twice a week? Is that normal?"

"Yes, Metyu. In the old buildings, many do not have tanks. New buildings do. But not in this neighborhood—it's very old. So people save the water when it is coming."

I may not have been surprised when Ayten raised the price of the room, but I was very surprised now. True, the building had seen better days. But, again, it was in the heart of Istanbul, a mere stone's throw away from luxury hotels and foreign consulates. While it would have come as little surprise that the slums surrounding the city might lack basic essentials such as reliable water, it never would have occurred to me that might be true just off Istanbul's main square. It was like renting a room off the Champs Elysées in Paris and discovering it only had electricity a few hours a day. I had expected Ayten's apartment to be an upgrade from where I was staying before. Apparently instead, it was to be the next step in my cultural immersion, firsthand exposure to day-to-day challenges about which I'd been completely ignorant until now.

"Oh. Well, OK, cool. But then how do I shower? I mean, on days when there's no water."

Neşe had another quick exchange with Ayten. The old lady had a deep, raspy voice. I couldn't smell it in the apartment, but she had to be a smoker.

"Ayten *hanım* says that in the kitchen you heat the water. Then you take it down the hall to the bathroom."

In other words, when there was no water, you didn't shower. Or even bathe—not in the way I was accustomed, at least. Not in the way, for that matter, my Turkish friends who lived in more recent neighborhoods were accustomed either.

Instead, you overlooked the fact that, in a culture that traditionally held its bathing rituals in such high esteem it had exported them to the far reaches of a long-since-expired empire, you couldn't be sure if or when you'd bathe at all. You made do the best you could, spot-cleaning the critical areas—adding a few extra coats of deodorant, for good measure—until storm clouds again gathered in the bathroom, and the shower rained down once more.

It didn't help that I moved into the apartment in the middle of winter.

As I had learned on my initial visit, the apartment didn't have central heat. Each bedroom had its own space heater. There wasn't one in the water closet or bathroom, so I spent as little time as possible in both. Still, I couldn't avoid them altogether.

The first time I had to bathe without water from the tap was a brutally cold morning. Groggy eyed, my body still heavy with slumber, I stumbled into the kitchen. I found a large pot, filled it with water from one of the plastic containers, and put it on the stove. Sitting down at the kitchen table, I glided my fingers across the brightly colored, fancifully patterned plastic covering. Ayten had missed a spot, and my hand was ensnared in a gooey patch of honey.

I understood the practical benefits of covering a table in plastic, but I never liked it. It seemed like a cheap, even desperate, attempt at avoiding the inevitable. Things—whether books or cars or furniture—were made for a purpose. They were meant to be used. Over time, they would wear out. If they were taken care of, they would last longer, they would fulfill their reasons for being that much more dutifully. In the process, they would acquire character, and they would become valued even more for it. Wasn't that preferable to sitting idle, wrapped in plastic, doted over to the point of being useless, like the living room furniture in so many American homes in the '50s and '60s? Wasn't that a glaring metaphor for our own lives, for what we stand to lose by playing it safe or, hopefully, gain by taking risks?

Returning from my rumination, I remembered I needed to wash some socks. I had worn my last clean pair the day before and, unless I wanted to wear one of my dirty pairs a second time—not an option, when you have feet as sweaty as mine—I had to wash some ASAP.

I got up from the table and stepped back across the hall. I grabbed a dirty pair of socks, returned to the kitchen and, as the water in the pot continued to heat up, I gave the socks a quick wash in the sink. I then ran back to my bedroom and lay the socks over the top of the space heater—vowing not to forget they were there. There wasn't a dryer in the apartment, so I didn't have any other way of drying the socks before I went out for the day.

Back in the kitchen, I looked at the water on the stove. Little bubbles were forming at the bottom, and a faint vapor was just starting to take to the air. I turned off the gas and picked up the pot. Being careful not to rush, not to send water spilling over the sides, I carried the pot down the long hall to the bathroom and set it in the tub.

The bathroom was so cold, I thought about just taking off my shirt and limiting my efforts to the waist up. But I hadn't showered the day before either. I didn't want to be asked to leave school later that day because I stank.

I let my pants fall to the floor.

Ordinarily, the room would have been warmed by steam from the shower. Now the only heat source was less than a gallon of hot—not even boiling—water. I had to get this over and done with.

I put a towel on the floor and kneeled over the side of the tub, as though to say a quick prayer before my unorthodox variation on the bathing ritual. The mood in the room vaguely recalled that of a place of worship, after all. Or, perhaps, it was more like a prison cell. There were no windows. A single, weak light bulb cast a dim, grayish light. The room was old, and it felt old. The fixtures were dated, probably antique, hints of rust around their edges. Peeling paint on the ceiling curled back like wood shavings. Random tiles were chipped, and here and there duct tape held things together, barely. The room, like the rest of the apartment, felt as though it had passed a point of no return, resigned itself to a slow and steady decline; a chronic decline.

I leaned forward. My body recoiled when it came into contact with the chilled porcelain. My knees hurt against the hard surface of the floor—the towel not enough of a buffer—so I adjusted, moving them into a more comfortable position. I put my hand into the pot, making sure the water wasn't too hot. Then, as though bobbing for apples, I stuck my head into it, far enough to get as much of my hair wet as possible.

The contrast between the welcome warmth dripping down my head—my eyes closed, as I reached blindly for the shampoo—and the frigid cold assaulting the rest of my body was confusing, a beguiling combination of pleasure and pain. I washed my hair quickly, feeling a little better, as the hot water dripped down onto my shoulders and chest.

Moving on to my pits, I kept a vigilant eye on how much water I was using. I had to ration it carefully, unless I wanted to go all the way back to the kitchen and heat up another pot.

There was something else I was supposed to be keeping a vigilant eye on.

A wave of panic shot through my body, more chilling than the icy porcelain against my torso. I jumped up, toweled myself off as quickly as I could, and bolted down the hall.

Throwing open the door to my room, my eyes went straight for the space heater. Neither it nor the socks were aflame. My fears, however, were not unfounded. The heat from the electric coils had burnt a hole through each sock. Both holes were not only slowly expanding, but emitting faint wisps into the air. It was only a matter of time—and a very short one at that—before the socks caught fire. Followed by the room. Followed by the apartment. Followed by the building, which was just one in a very densely packed neighborhood of many.

Before long, Istanbul would be burning.

It was the last time I used the space heater as a clothes dryer.

My heart still racing, I went back out into the hall and stepped inside the water closet. After taking a few deep breaths, I relieved myself. When the time came to flush, I didn't.

There was no running water here, either.

I filled a bucket with water from the reserves and dumped it into the toilet. It flushed.

It struck me as curious that it was that simple. Each time. Flushing with a bucket had done away with any mystique enshrouding the porcelain god. Until my time in Istanbul, I'd never given much thought to how it worked. Now, I couldn't help but feel that something so essential to our day-to-day lives should be more complicated. At the very least, it should have some sort of mechanization, something beyond a hand-operated lever. It should use electricity. In these technology-obsessed times, it should probably have a chip. Perhaps even data-gathering, backup-storage, and rectal-recognition technology.

Living without reliable water had at least one more noteworthy consequence: during my several months in the apartment, I developed a superhuman attunement to the building's water pipes. Like an animal that senses an earthquake long before the ground begins to tremble, whenever the first drop of water began to flow into the building—regardless of the hour—I was wide awake. Before I knew it, I was halfway down the hall and in the shower, in time for that very first drop to fall upon my naked body.

If I ever took water for granted before living in Istanbul, I never have since.

15 A DIRE MISCALCULATION

I had rescued Sunny in the Cairo airport. A tall, lanky, blond-and-blue-eyed Australian, like me at the time, he was in his mid-twenties. Unlike me, he didn't have six months under his belt living on the mean streets of a semi-developing country. He lacked my experience dealing with belligerent, pestering touts.

Like hyenas sensing a kill, a mob had surrounded him, recognizing a perfect victim to drag to the hotel or store or wherever else would reward them with a handsome bounty for his head. Without giving it a second thought, I broke through the chaos, grabbed Sunny by the hand, and took him with me to a cab. Shell-shocked and grateful, he offered no resistance.

That was a week earlier. We'd been traveling together ever since.

Making our way south, we had arrived in Luxor. Although tempted to go all the way to Aswan, we opted instead to catch a *felucca*—a wooden sailboat traditionally used on the Nile—to head back north.

In the months preceding our arrival, there had been a few "incidents" targeting tourists. Rules had since been implemented to prevent further loss of life—and dollars. One such regulation required a minimum number of foreign passengers on a felucca. I guess the idea was that there be enough foreigners to overpower any locals with ulterior motives. It didn't seem like particularly sound logic. I couldn't help but think that locals taking foreigners into the middle of nowhere by boat had the advantage, regardless of the math.

Sunny and I searched the vicinity of the docks high and low, but were unable to find any other travelers ready to depart. When the felucca "captain" saw that our prospects weren't looking good, he made a suggestion: we could sneak out of town without alerting the authorities.

In addition to the captain, there was one other crew member. Both seemed like nice young men. Their dark skin suggested sub-Saharan Africa, but their facial features looked Arab. They wore white cotton garments, and had broad smiles and calm, good-natured demeanors. They felt trustworthy. There was no pressure, no wheeling and dealing. It was just an offer, one potentially beneficial to everyone involved—assuming no kidnapping, extortion, or murder. The Egyptians would get clients; we would get to start our trip without delay.

We had a deal.

As the sun went down, Sunny and I found ourselves lying in the bottom of a felucca, looking up at the twilight sky. Whereas most people take delight in watching the shore retreat, in observing the change in perspective as the boat takes to the currents, all we saw were stars setting foot onstage. All of us—Sunny and I, as well as the two Egyptians—hoped that neither a watchman on the shore nor a patrol boat on the water would catch on to our covert escape. I didn't bother to ask what would happen if they did.

They didn't.

The next day was extraordinary. We were sailing on the Nile. The same Nile we'd heard so much about as children in Sunday school. The mythic river that sustained an entire nation—not to mention ancient civilizations before it—turning sandy desert shores into fertile countryside. A river bordered by celebrated pyramids, temples, and tombs, inhabited by crocodiles almost as legendary. A river that, even now, from our perspective in the middle of it, seemed to flow through a time and place all its own.

The shores were often covered with lush vegetation, grasses, bushes, and small trees crowding each other for access to the water. In other places there was nothing but sand. Sometimes there were flat fields, sometimes steep mountains. Towering palms were common, entire stands of them occasionally sheltering dwellings made of adobe. Again I was reminded of Biblical times. As far as I could tell, the simple earthen structures were built in the same manner as they had been for millennia.

The same might have been said for our felucca. For all its charm, it did not have a toilet. We, therefore, did not have an option; if we had to go, we had to stop. Besides being ecologically irresponsible, defecating over the side of the boat would have been challenging at best, dangerous at worst. It was also likely to seriously piss off some crocodiles.

Under ordinary conditions, we could have gone several hours without relieving ourselves. As is so often the case when traveling, however, these were not ordinary conditions.

Upon my arrival in Turkey many months earlier, I had suffered through sixteen days of diarrhea. It hadn't been pretty. The upside was that I now had a gut made of steel. Or, almost. Apparently Egypt had introduced some new microbes into my system; and, while not as vicious as those I had encountered in Turkey, they had nonetheless loosened things up. Limited vegetarian options on the road hadn't helped—particularly given that one of my dietary staples was figs. On the boat, we were practically living on them, fresh, healthy, high-fiber figs. It was sort of like binging on laxatives when we should have been guzzling Imodium.

Neither Sunny nor I wanted to be responsible for asking our hosts to pull over. After all, "pulling over" a sailboat on a river that's an average of two miles wide is a little more involved than pulling a car over to the side of a road. We were in the middle of nowhere. We couldn't just stop at the nearest dock. They were few and far between.

An unspoken high-stakes brinkmanship ensued. Sunny and I each worked hard to disregard our respective needs, in the hopes the other's would become unbearable first.

Sweat soon covered my brow. It wasn't the desert heat. It was evidence of my silent suffering. It was the fear of a familiar rumbling on my insides, a foreboding like an approaching storm. It was mounting anxiety as I strained to hear signs of similar distress coming from Sunny's gut, praying his would shortly become more intolerable than my own. It was grave concern for a sphincter fast approaching its limits, the tension of sitting on a powder keg about to blow—without knowing when. It was futile resistance to a truth that could no longer be ignored.

This was not going to end well.

"You doing okay, mate?" Sunny asked.

"Oh, yeah, I feel great."

"Are you sure? You look a little pale ..."

"No, don't think so—must be the sunshine. It's so bright."

"Yeah, must be."

"You've be keeping pretty quiet, though. You feeling alright?"

"Who me? Oh, yeah, you know—just enjoying the scenery."

"Yeah."

An awkward pause followed.

"You sure haven't eaten much today," Sunny observed, his tone forced. "How 'bout a fig?"

Sunny offered me the bowl.

I swallowed hard.

"Oh, no, it's cool. Thanks, but I'm good."

"You sure? You really need to eat—we're sweating out lots of minerals. Got to keep your energy up."

He offered me the bowl again, looking me deep in the eyes. Probing.

I hesitated. But I didn't want to let on to the truth.

I took a fig.

"Just one?" Sunny insisted, still holding out the bowl.

I don't remember who finally gave in. What I do remember is that, as far as Sunny and I were concerned, our little felucca couldn't get to shore fast enough. The proud white sail, harkening back to another time, now became a disturbing reminder we were almost out of it. I would have given anything to dispense with tradition and throw the engine into full throttle. But there wasn't a throttle. Or even an engine. So, our reunion with dry land happened in tortuous slow motion, my innards a bubbling cauldron, my sphincter a gasket about to blow.

Scarcely had we touched sand, than Sunny and I were off the boat, each scrambling in different directions in search of some privacy.

We had stopped in a wild area of small dunes and clumps of tall grasses. There was no agriculture, no dwellings. My feet were buffered by the soft ground, but there was still the inevitable impact each time they fell upon it. I had only run a short distance when I knew I was in trouble.

I'd been on the verge for too long. It was a miracle my body had withstood the pressure for as long as it had. Deluding myself into thinking it could do so while running— no matter how short the distance—was a dire miscalculation.

As I desperately scanned the environs for a place to relieve myself, my foot came down on the sand just a little too hard. That was all it took. My sphincter lost its grip, and I lost my race against time.

Out streamed digested figs. If I'd been a bird, I would have dispersed enough seeds to plant an orchard.

I couldn't believe it.

I felt defeated. I felt embarrassed. I felt really stupid.

I also felt no small amount of disgust. The ordeal, after all, was far from over. I was covered in it.

What now? Not having shat myself since graduating from diapers to underpants, the situation was a novel one. The fact that I had no way of washing myself made it that much more of a challenge.

There was also the question of what to do with my soiled

polka dot boxers. I hated the thought of leaving them behind. If I did, I'd be adding to the mementos shamelessly left by countless other travelers. Our felucca was far from the first to recognize in the spot a good stopping point. The sand was strewn with used toilet paper.

Dreading each mushy step I took, I found a patch of dune afforded some privacy by a wall of tall grass. I took off my pants. Again I was overcome with disbelief. I may not have felt shame wearing diapers as a toddler, but I abhorred what essentially amounted to changing my own now. I would have killed for some wet wipes. A little talcum powder would have been life-changing. Instead, carefully using unsoiled sections of each leg of the boxers, I made do the best I could. Thank god I hadn't been wearing briefs.

I had to face yet another uncomfortable truth. My boxers were now covered in filth. The only way to hold them was with my index finger and thumb pinching one of the few remaining clean spots, my arm extended. There was no way around it: I had to leave my boxers behind.

That did not mean, however, that I had to leave them in plain sight. Even if I was one of only a few who bothered, to the extent possible, I didn't want to leave any trace.

With both hands, I dug a hole. It felt like preparing for a funeral for someone unjustly sentenced to death—and unable to afford a proper burial. It didn't seem fair. Given their selfless sacrifice, my martyred boxers deserved better. Like the Pharaohs memorialized in these very lands, they were worthy of their own tomb, of an elaborate sarcophagus, vivid murals, and at least one mummified cat.

Once the hole was deep enough, with heavy heart, I dropped my boxers into its sandy depths. Holding back tears, I thought about all the shit we'd been through together. I offered some words of thanks and said a brief prayer to facilitate their transition to the afterlife. I then refilled the hole.

It occurred to me as I threw in the last handful of sand that never would I have imagined one day burying my underwear on the banks of the Nile.

Making my way back to the felucca, although I still struggled with shame and disgust, I felt tremendous physical relief. Any feelings of uncleanliness on the outside were far outweighed by the menacing pressure having been released from my insides. I felt lighter, possessed of a renewed calm.

Until I looked ahead, down the interminable length of the mighty river.

This was not going to end well.

16 YOU CALLED ME A GIRL

When Mickey invited me on an overnight kayaking trip in Tomales Bay, I jumped at the chance.

Along with two of his friends, we would paddle across the bay, camp on a small beach, and paddle back the next morning. An hour and a half north of San Francisco, Tomales Bay was one of my favorite places. I'd never been kayaking there. I was excited about the opportunity.

Tall, with a pale, pockmarked complexion and a full head of blond hair on its way to becoming silver, Mickey was a tech entrepreneur who lived in Noe Valley, one of San Francisco's most affluent neighborhoods. When he wasn't zipping around town in his blue BMW roadster, Mickey was pedaling up and down the mean streets of the city on his bike. I never understood how he pulled it off in the tight, expensive jeans he always wore. His polos were less form-fitting, allowing some breathing room for the few extra pounds that filled out his thick torso. Designer frames completed the picture, and ensured Mickey saw oncoming traffic.

In his early fifties, Mickey's online dating profile claimed he was in his mid-forties. "The last girl I dated said she wouldn't have gone out with me if she had known my real age," he justified. They were no longer together.

I had only hung out one-on-one with Mickey a couple of times. We had met at a party thrown by our mutual friend Sandra, shortly before she moved overseas. Any friend of Sandra's is a friend of mine, and I'm always open to making new connections—especially since San Francisco is so transient, Sandra just one on a long list of close friends who have left it behind. On the other hand, I hadn't felt a particularly strong kinship with Mickey. He was nice enough, but he was also high-strung and hard to read. All the same, flattered when he reached out after Sandra moved away, I opened myself to the possibility of a new friendship.

It hadn't taken long for me to begin questioning how close Mickey and I would become. My doubts started with the hash browns.

One Sunday Mickey had suggested we have brunch. We met in front of the restaurant, Mickey locked up his bike, and we went inside. The restaurant was a casual, neighborhood one. It didn't have waiters. We ordered at the counter.

The space itself was light and airy, big windows in front, a set of doors in back opening onto a large, leafy patio. The interior floor appeared to be the original hardwood, the ceiling was covered in decorative pressed tin. Like every weekend morning, a line of hungry hipsters trailed out the door.

Things were going more or less as expected until the hash browns arrived. The hash browns, it turned out, were not up to muster.

"Hey, you know, I'm really sorry," Mickey began, addressing our food runner, Luis. Luis was about 5'5", with a small but solid frame. He had exceptionally smooth skin, big brown eyes, and full lips. Sweat on his brow, he ran from the kitchen to the dining room and back again, over and over, scarcely pausing to catch his breath.

"But for me," Mickey continued, "hash browns need to be a little crispier? You know what I mean?"

Luis nodded. He barely spoke English, but he got the point. No questions asked, he picked up Mickey's plate to take it back to the kitchen. Before he could go anywhere, though, Mickey stopped him.

Mickey had more to say.

"It's just, well, you see, these are clearly somewhat crispy, but only on the surface," he explained, picking up his fork and poking at the hash browns, like at an animal he wanted to confirm was dead. "The crispiness should go a little deeper—but not too deep, right? I mean, I'm definitely not saying they should be overcooked."

Luis nodded again. I began to feel bad for him. I wouldn't have been surprised if he only understood half of what Mickey was saying. And whatever he was paid, it wasn't nearly enough to be forced to listen to a lecture on the art of the perfect hash brown.

Mickey didn't see it that way.

"So, you get where I'm coming from, right? You understand why I'd like them sent back? Probably just another couple of minutes—I don't think I'd do much more than that—and I bet they'll be just right. Could you please explain that to the cook?"

Luis nodded yet again. He was beginning to look like a bobble-head doll.

In addition to feeling bad for him, I now felt guilty by association. It didn't bother me that Mickey liked his hash browns a certain way. He was a paying customer. If something wasn't to his satisfaction, he was entitled to say so. What made me uncomfortable, even a little embarrassed, was his presumption that Luis would have any interest in grasping every last detail of Mickey's first-world problem.

Perhaps if it hadn't been the first time I'd been witness to such an interaction, it might not have bothered me as much. But it wasn't the first time. It was my second brunch with Mickey, and it was the second in-depth discussion about why he was sending back potatoes.

※

Mickey and his friends Peter and Tricia, a married couple, showed up at my place early Saturday morning. Both in their early forties, Peter worked for a start-up in Silicon Valley; Tricia worked in Finance in a skyscraper downtown. So clean-cut I was tempted to rub their skin to see if they squeaked, both were warm and friendly as I loaded my camping gear into their late-model Lexus SUV.

Peter and Tricia fit right in with the latest wave of ambitious, professional transplants drawn West by a dot-com gold rush that—despite briefly lurching to a calamitous halt—continued to generate inestimable wealth. I took it as a given we'd be talking about stock options, IPOs, and the latest tech-industry buzz.

Or, rather, they would.

I didn't know it yet, but I wasn't supposed to talk.

As we crossed the Golden Gate Bridge, I paused to take in the view. I'd seen it countless times before. It didn't matter. Each time was different. Sunny or foggy, bright-blue or misty-gray. I always marveled at the tumultuous waters far below. Inevitably my eyes were drawn to Alcatraz, the big rock holding its own amidst sailboats and commuter ferries crisscrossing the bay. I looked ahead with anticipation as we approached the first art deco tower—international orange, not gold—followed shortly after by the second.

Just beyond the far end of the suspension, the green, gold, and red of the headlands rose up like a wall fortifying southern Marin county. I contemplated the low-lying vegetation, the single-lane road winding down to the lighthouse, the rocky cliffs eroding into the ocean.

As we continued north toward Tomales Bay, the mood in the car was lively. Everyone was excited and upbeat as our adventure got underway. Casual conversation gave way to witty banter. We were all enjoying ourselves. Our interaction had an easy, natural flow.

Until Mickey began to talk over me.

At first it was no big deal. It hardly even registered. And when it did, I simply chalked it up to his enthusiasm, to the excitement in the car. All in good fun.

"You know," I commented, when Tricia pointed out a small flock of pelicans flying over the car, "they're actually endangered—"

"Come on!" Mickey blurted out, before I could finish my thought. "They look like pterodactyls! If they've managed to survive this long, I'm sure they'll be fine."

Not only was his comment callous, it was odd, coming out of nowhere. Unsure what to make of it, I let it go.

Shortly after, Peter mentioned that he and Tricia were planning a trip to Spain, somewhere I've both lived and traveled extensively.

"I love Barcelona. If you decide to go, you really should—"

"Barcelona is so overrated!" Mickey interjected, once again cutting me off. "Madrid is way more interesting."

I had given Mickey the benefit of the doubt. He'd had too much coffee. He was only trying to make himself heard. Now, though, he was no longer merely talking over me. He was cutting me off, silencing me. His tone had taken on a certain edge, a subtle but unmistakable aggression directed toward me—but not Peter or Tricia. When Mickey began subtly mocking things I said, I knew I wasn't imagining things.

I know how to engage in conversation. I know how to strike a balance between participating and letting others speak. Peter and Tricia were Mickey's friends. For all I knew, I'd never see them again after our weekend together—I had no interest in impressing or somehow ingratiating myself to them. I was just trying to be a good sport and have a good time. I didn't want to be a bump on a log. Neither did I have any need to be the center of attention.

Mickey did.

Perhaps I should have seen it coming, considering the spoiled little boy he became when served undercooked potatoes. But I didn't. I'd never been with Mickey around his friends. I had no way of knowing beforehand, but now it was clear: this was his show. If I had been invited along, it wasn't as an actor; it was as a spectator. It didn't matter how much Peter and Tricia talked or joked or gave him a hard time. They were members of the club. I was a newcomer, an outsider. Mickey was intent on making sure I knew my place—and didn't forget it.

I got the hint and toned it down. Rather than actively engage in the conversation—show interest, ask questions, make jokes—like a good geisha, I assumed the role expected of me. I smiled and nodded and laughed on cue. I stopped being myself.

It was going to be a very long weekend.

Tomales Bay is a unique body of water. Much longer than it is wide, the infamous San Andreas fault runs down its middle. Located on the North American tectonic plate, the eastern shore of the bay is characterized by large, rolling hills of grassy pasture, green in the spring, straw-gold the rest of the year. The western shore, which is on the Pacific plate, is within easy view, a long, forested mountain ridge rising up like a dike, holding back the ocean on the other side.

Any underlying tectonic tension was indiscernible as we pulled into the kayak rental parking lot. The sky was a perfect blue, no sign of the fog that often hovers over the bay. Other than squawking seagulls and the occasional soaring vulture, the only thing in the air was warm sunshine. It was welcome.

Peter went into the rental office to check in. A couple of other small groups had arrived before us. We'd have to wait our turn to get assigned kayaks and gear.

In the meantime, after an hour and a half in the car, Mickey needed to go to the bathroom. He was standing in front of three Porta Pottis, yet he looked confused, anxious even.

"You realize there are three toilets right behind you?" I asked, smiling. I assumed he had overlooked them.

"Yeah, I know, but ..." His voice trailed off as he

continued looking around, increasingly agitated. Tricia and I exchanged looks. What was wrong with Mickey?

One of the staff members came out of the office. Little more than a large wooden shack, its blue paint was peeling from a never-ending assault by the elements, the wind, water, and sun each taking their unforgiving toll on the battered but resilient structure.

"Hey, excuse me, are there any other bathrooms?" Mickey asked. His voice was almost pained.

The guy, a rugged twenty-something with an unkempt beard, wild light-brown hair, and a deep tan, looked Mickey up and down. He then responded matter-of-factly, "Nope. Just those."

"What's wrong with the Porta-Jons?" asked Peter, once the staff member had gone to help some customers choose life jackets.

"I don't know … I just hate Porta-Jons," Mickey whined.

"You realize we're going camping, right?" Tricia teased, as she took a drink from her water bottle.

"Yeah, do you need a bidet or what?" I quipped.

Before I knew what hit me, Mickey had. In the arm. Hard. He did it under the pretense of a joke, but he wasn't laughing. Neither was I. It hurt.

"Damn, Mickey!" Peter reacted. My own reaction must have confirmed his suspicions: Mickey really had hit me as hard as it seemed.

"Yeah, a little uptight this morning?" Tricia teased, her eyes darting from Mickey to me and back again. She almost looked afraid of what might happen next.

"I just don't like Porta-Jons," Mickey repeated, seemingly on the verge of a tantrum—and refusing to acknowledge what he had done.

I said nothing. I was still processing what had happened. I didn't want to respond to his rash, aggressive gesture with one of my own. I didn't want to react without thinking first, only to regret it. I needed to regroup. I needed to make sense of the situation and consider the circumstances.

We hadn't even gotten our kayaks yet. Our adventure, most of which would be spent in very close quarters on a tiny stretch of beach, had barely gotten underway. We'd be spending almost every moment together, in the kayaks, in the tents, in the car the next day. Did I really want to make a big deal about Mickey's reflexive blunder? He was an idiot for having hit me as hard as he had, but surely he hadn't meant to. Right? And again, unless I wanted to hitchhike back to the City, for the next twenty-four hours I was stuck with him.

Just like I'd just taken one in the arm, I decided to take one for the team. Rather than make things more awkward, I let it go.

I wasn't looking forward to sharing a tent.

My stiff arm notwithstanding, kayaking across the bay was spectacular. Ospreys flew overhead, fish in their talons silver in the sunlight. Two seals appeared out of nowhere to see what the humans were up to. The ever-changing perspective as one shore retreated and another approached was a constant source of curiosity and inspiration.

It helped that we each had our own kayaks. I was able to keep my distance from the juvenile adult who had not only silenced but—adding injury to insult—accosted me.

Once we reached the beach, setting up camp proved a welcome focus for our collective energies. When we had some time on our hands before dinner, I wandered off on my own, happy to explore the far end of the beach, the tide pools and whatever else I might stumble upon. In addition to Mickey's lunacy, I had grown weary of pleasant chit-chat with strangers. I relished the time on my own, recharged by my solitude and the surroundings.

I spied a sleek white egret just down the shore, standing motionless as it readied its razor-like beak to stab an unsuspecting fish. A gentle breeze in my face, a salty taste on my lips, I gazed across the bay to golden hills set against a cloudless blue sky. Waters lapped the shore at my feet, the briny scent of kelp suffused the air, and a light bruise slowly took form on my arm.

The sun low in the sky, I wandered back to camp. Dinner came soon after, followed by a couple of hours around the fire. Rather than say too much, I mostly just listened.

Mickey seemed pleased with my behavior, reassured perhaps, now that I was no longer a threat. Having put me in my place, my brief turn as foe had passed; from his perspective, we were once again pals.

I didn't see it that way.

We got settled in our tent. Mickey was as upbeat as if he'd just been served a perfect plate of potatoes. We chatted for a while, before eventually nodding off.

Or, rather, before he nodded off.

I struggled to fall asleep because, rather than stick to his side of the tent, Mickey was in the middle of it—pushing me into the nylon wall on my side. *Am I imagining things?* I wondered. I got up on one arm, looking over Mickey's unconscious body, rising and falling with each laborious breath. No, there was plenty of room on his side, almost enough for a third person. The tent was not a small one.

I wasn't going to get any sleep with my face pressed against the wall. I gently tried to nudge Mickey back toward his side.

Yet again, I miscalculated.

Out of nowhere came a shove that was strikingly powerful and precise for someone allegedly fast asleep.

Once more, I was blindsided.

What was wrong with this guy? I knew he was eccentric. What I hadn't realized was that he was also prone to acting out.

"Mickey," I said angrily. "Mickey, you are practically on top of me. Can you please move over to your side of the tent?"

He grunted and obliged.

The next morning, I was the first one up. I was the first to finish breakfast. I was the first to load my things into my kayak. I had my sights set on one thing, and one thing alone: getting the hell off the beach and back to the other side of the bay.

As soon as everyone else caught up with me, that's exactly what we did.

On the ride back to the City, I didn't even feign interest in the conversation. I pretended to be tired, and just let Mickey talk—which he was exceedingly happy to do. I no longer cared what he or his friends thought of me.

I was done.

Mickey called a couple of days later to check in. To his credit, he knew that things had soured between us, and he wanted to talk about it. To his discredit, he neither acknowledged nor apologized for being a hostile, out-of-line ass.

When it was clear he had no intention of owning up to hitting me, I called him on it.

"But you called me a girl!" he shouted, suddenly defensive.

At last. Days later, it finally made sense. A fifty-two-year-old man had physically assaulted me because I had called him a girl. An ostensibly progressive, longtime resident of San Francisco had been so offended by my associating him with the opposite gender, he had felt justified in hitting me so hard I was sore the next day.

I couldn't help but wonder what exactly it was about being a girl—or a woman—that Mickey found so insulting. I might have expected it from an elementary-school boy, the kind who thinks girls are gross. But from a full-grown adult?

There was something even stranger still.

I hadn't called him a girl.

"Mickey, what are you talking about? I never called you a girl."

The words felt odd coming from my mouth. They didn't

feel like my own. They felt like something I'd been force-fed and had to vomit back up. Mickey had dragged me back to the playground with him.

"Yes, you did!" he retorted.

Wow.

"Ah, no, Mickey, honestly. I never called you a girl."

"Yes, you did!" He was adamant, getting more worked up. "You said I used a bidet!"

Thank god we were on the phone. If Mickey had seen my reaction, I have little doubt he would have tried to pummel me.

So that's what this was about?

Mickey needed to spend more time in Europe. Or Japan. Or at a rich American's house. His understanding of bidets was sorely lacking, and I now found myself faced with the ever-so-delicate task of filling him in. The challenge was not to further offend his ever-so-delicate ego.

"Mickey, I think there's been a misunderstanding."

"So you didn't mean it?"

"No, it's not that. It's that … well, bidets aren't only used by women."

"What do you mean? Yes they are! They use them to clean their vaginas!"

Oh boy.

"Well, yeah, maybe. I mean, probably. What I mean is that bidets are used for whatever hygienic purpose a person needs to use them for—man or woman. They're just used to get water up into those hard-to-reach places."

Mickey said nothing, wheels turning.

"You mean like after going to the bathroom?"

"Exactly."

"So they're not just for women?"

"Nope."

Mickey paused again.

"Then you really weren't calling me a girl, were you?"

"Nope."

More silence, as the final pieces came together for him.

"I'm sorry. I guess I was a real prick, wasn't I?"

"Yep."

I appreciated Mickey calling to talk things through. I appreciated his apology. But the damage was done. I'd seen and heard too much. And then, of course, being hit and shoved failed to ease my concerns. I was willing to let bygones be bygones. Embarrassed I'd put up with as much from him as I had, however, I was not willing to set myself up for more of the same.

Our budding friendship had died on the vine.

17 IDENTITY CRISIS

After hours of arid mountains and deep-blue sea, orange groves began appearing on both sides of the tracks. Soon the train was traveling through vast expanses of them, orange trees for as far as the eye could see.

We had arrived in Valencia.

Having spent a year in Valencia as an exchange student and returned many times since, I was on home turf. Without pausing to get my bearings, I threaded my way through the crowds in the art deco train station—it, too, covered in oranges—and headed down into the subway. Not long after, I was back above ground, back in my old neighborhood a mere block from my friends' apartment.

The trip from Barcelona had been uneventful. All the same, it was summer in Spain. Moving between modes of transportation meant stepping into the blinding sun and sweltering heat. I was a sticky mess. I really needed a shower.

My friends had made the curious choice of decorating their bathroom in a black and white checkerboard style that seemed likely to induce flashbacks of drugs I'd never done. And it wasn't just the floor tiles. Black and white squares covered the walls. A black and white spiral graced the ceiling. It was surreal. It was unlikely to win any design awards.

Despite the danger of an imminent seizure, my attention shifted to more immediate concerns. The bathroom had not only a shower, but a full-size bathtub. What it did not have, for whatever reason—as I suddenly remembered from my previous visit—was a shower curtain.

It had been a while, but this was far from the first time I'd been in a European bathroom with a shower lacking a curtain. I'd never understood why, and I still don't. How do they do it? How would I do it? Could I shower without getting water all over the bathroom, without having a floor to mop? It seemed difficult at best. But I didn't want to take a bath. I just wanted to get in and get out.

I lowered myself into the tub and turned on the water, triggering the familiar roar as the tankless hot-water heater ignited. What had I done last time? Again I wondered what my friends did. I knew they didn't take a full-on bath every time they bathed. Maybe they took a shower standing up, in spite of the lack of a curtain, and just mopped up afterwards, as I had conservatively decided against? Maybe they sat in the tub without filling it, taking a sitting shower? Or, maybe they got on their haunches? Whatever it was, wouldn't it have been a thousand times easier just to buy a shower curtain? Since they hadn't, I got down on my haunches.

It was the only option that seemed to make sense. But it was hard work.

Holding the unusual position put an uncomfortable strain on my back, legs, and feet. It was even more challenging given that I had an unruly metal hose on my hands. It refused to sit still. When I needed to get some shampoo, I set down the showerhead with the utmost of care, like putting a sleeping baby into its crib. Only once I was absolutely certain it was resting in a stable position, did I take my hands off it.

Despite showing every indication of being in the deepest, most blissful of slumbers, a mere moment later the showerhead burst into a tear-laden tantrum. Without warning it began thrashing from side to side. Before I could stop it, it flipped onto its back. Now subsumed in a full-blown identity crisis, it mistook itself for a lawn sprinkler. Water shot sky-high, ending up everywhere—including on the ceiling. From there it fell back down on me, tauntingly, mocking my ineptitude, drop by drop.

I would be mopping the floor after all.

And wiping down the sink and toilet and everything else the showerhead thought should be covered in lush green grass.

I never really got the hang of bathing in Valencia. When I managed not to make a mess, I felt as though I hadn't really showered. When I took a thorough, satisfying shower, I ended up turning the bathroom into a water park. There had to be some middle ground.

I never found it.

18 NOW YOU SEE IT, NOW YOU DON'T

The bathroom was right there when I opened the front door. So much the better, since I really needed to pee.

I had arrived in Oslo after a pleasant, six-hour train ride from Stockholm. Oslo was just a stopover on my way to the fjords; so, rather than get my own place, I had rented a room for the night in a Norwegian woman's flat. My host wasn't home, but she had left the keys at the pizza place downstairs. I let myself in.

About three times as long as it was wide—not more than four feet from side to side—a bright-white porcelain tunnel opened up before me. It ended at a toilet and a minuscule sink.

I stepped inside and walked toward the toilet. There was no tub, but there was a shower. At least I thought there was a shower. Taking a casual look, I had to do a double-take—my eyes seemed to be playing tricks on me. Through a set of glass doors, I expected to see a stall. What I saw instead was a wall.

The wall was set back about six inches, creating a shallow recess. There was a heart-shaped showerhead, as well as a small shelf with a bottle of neon-pink shower gel. Perhaps this was the shower, after all.

But how was it possible to bathe in a space only six inches deep? Even if I sucked in my gut and held my breath, there was little chance I'd fit. Never mind have any hope of closing the doors. Never mind move.

I took a closer look. There wasn't just one set of doors; there were two. Since it, too, was transparent, I hadn't noticed the second set, which was located right behind the first.

My eyes followed the small space between the doors to the floor. A square area sunk about an inch lower than the rest of the tiles. The entire floor was the same pattern, so initially the sunken area did not stand out.

It all began to make sense.

I opened the first set of doors, pulling them outward. The rubber flap on the bottom of each protested like a squeegee dragging across tile, until the doors reached the left and right sides, respectively, of the depression in the floor. At the same time, the second set of doors swung slightly inward, offering me a clue as to what came next. It was then that I realized they were connected to the first. There weren't two sets of doors, after all; rather, there was just one, each of which had two panes that folded together.

I took hold of the second set of panes, and brought them toward me. As they came forward, the last side of the square took form. I now had before me an enclosed glass compartment.

I also had before me my first pop-out shower.

Until then, I hadn't even known there was such a thing. It was ingenious.

I took off my clothes, got inside, and turned on the water, quickly forgetting that this shower was any different from the countless others in which I'd bathed.

Until I was done.

There was, after all, yet another difference.

I'd never had to fold up a shower after using it.

19 WATCHING YOU

A fawn I hadn't noticed paused to see who had joined her on the beach. A little wary but not afraid, she slowly walked away, eventually disappearing into the forest.

She wasn't the only one watching me.

But I didn't know that yet.

I was camping in a remote area of Northern California with two friends. I had woken up before them, and needed to go to the bathroom. We'd spent the night a short distance inland from a long, wide beach, the easiest place for me to do my business. I could do it far enough from the shore to avoid sullying the water.

The air was fresh, but it was much cooler than it had been the day before. The ocean, the sky, the mist, everything was gray. My eyes watering from peering into the cool wind, I looked out over the vast horizon, discerning nothing other than a subtle change in tone. Gentle waves lapped the shore. It was almost inconceivably serene.

Turning my attention to the matter at hand, I dug a hole in the sand. It was dark, thick and damp, with lots of tiny pebbles. It made a gritty, sloshing sound.

I pulled down my pants and squatted.

I couldn't help but be amused. I couldn't help but revel in

the irony of doing something so vulgar amidst such beauty. Of course, what I was doing fit perfectly into the natural order of things; in that sense, it wasn't so ironic after all. Still, it felt odd.

It also felt odd to defecate in such a wide-open space, probably the one and only time in my entire life that I didn't feel any need for discretion. It was strangely liberating, just me, the ocean, the clouds.

And the seal.

I gasped when I saw it. Not out of fear. Rather, because, lost in my solitary reverie, the last thing I expected was to find two huge, contemplative eyes smiling back at me.

The seal was as intrigued by me as I was by it. It was right there, as close as I could imagine it getting without coming ashore. And it was staring, staying right where it was, transfixed by the squatting human. It had probably never seen one before, not in that position, anyway.

I laughed. If before I had felt a sublime connection with my natural surroundings, I now felt an unlikely intimacy with my new friend. It was just the seal and I, sharing the moment, focused intensely on each other. He and I each finding our solitude abruptly interrupted by the unexpected appearance of a curious stranger.

I finished my business. The seal continued bobbing up and down in the water, observing my every move. It was only once I had buried my waste that he decided to be on his way. Perhaps that was the point. Perhaps he was making sure I cleaned up after myself, that I left the beach as I had found it.

Whatever his motives, I treasured our encounter.

20 OUT IN THE COLD

I got to the Nordic Countries a few days earlier than expected. I was living in Spain. My friend was in Finland. We were both high school exchange students. We had corresponded throughout the school year and, once it ended, I had purchased an Interrail train pass and headed north to see her.

Grateful for the extra time, I decided to take advantage of it. Rather than travel to Helsinki via Stockholm, which would have been much faster, from Copenhagen I would take a detour to Oslo. I'd then catch another train north, cut across the top of Sweden, and make my way down to Helsinki.

Other than mapping out my high-level route, I didn't do any planning. I didn't see the need. Thus far I'd been able to jump from train to train—including a few overnight ones—without much forethought, flashing my Interrail pass each time I boarded. More often than not, a reservation wasn't required. When I sometimes had a short or even a long wait, I hung around the station or took a walk. It was my first time traveling in Europe. Everything was new and exciting. I was enjoying a sort of freedom I'd never experienced, and I relished every moment of it.

If only I'd stopped to consider that travel in the Arctic Circle might not be quite as straightforward.

After a day roaming around Oslo, I caught the train north. What I remember most about the trip isn't the breathtaking scenery, the steep, rocky mountains, sometimes covered with forest, sometimes laid bare; the impeccably manicured farmland, everything perfectly in place; or the tumultuous white waters of the rivers, rushing alongside our train as though racing us to the next station. Rather, what made even more of an impression was how, after a certain point, we found ourselves immersed in a world of black and white.

I was fascinated. It was as though we'd left color to the south. All I saw was white snow and black rock. There was little or no vegetation, any green that might have enlivened the scene weathered into submission by the harsh arctic elements. Even the blue of the sky was covered with white, sometimes gray, occasionally black. It was another world.

Eventually I nodded off. When I woke up, something didn't feel right. Outside, the scenery continued to fly by, illuminated by the sun. Yet I couldn't escape the feeling I'd been sleeping for quite a while, that night should have fallen. I felt disoriented, as though trapped in that nebulous time in which dreams unfold, a time that might make sense or might not, a time bound by no rules. My disorientation was exacerbated by the sun, which had an unfamiliar quality; its strange hue almost seemed to suggest dusk had somehow been suspended.

I looked at my watch.

It was ten o'clock.

At night.

How was it possible, when the sun was still shining?

Then I remembered.

It was the third full week of June. I had traveled far enough north that, this time of year, the sun barely set. By the time I reached my destination further north, it wouldn't set at all.

Knowing I wasn't imagining things didn't make the situation any less surreal. It was as though my body knew better, but seeing the sun made it doubt itself. I felt physically fatigued, given that ordinarily my day would be winding down;

but, mentally I felt roused to life. The sun had driven a wedge between my mind and body, putting them at odds.

It was a couple of more hours before I stepped into the midnight sun. When I did, I was in for a rude awakening.

Just because the sun was shining, did not mean it was warm. I had made the same mistake so many tourists make in San Francisco. Thinking they're coming to warm and sunny California, they throw on their bathing suits, head to Ocean Beach, and plunge joyfully into the waves. Shocked by water as cold as a Finnish lake, they turn around and run back to shore, hoping to warm up. More often, they are subjected to a cold and relentless wind. The sun is shining, but they barely feel it. Wool sweaters, hot chocolate, and even a bonfire suddenly sound very appealing.

We had crossed the Arctic Circle hundreds of miles ago. It was freezing. Even still, the cold might not have been such a big deal, if it weren't for what I discovered when I checked the schedule on the platform.

There wasn't another train until morning.

My heart sank.

I was no longer in a big city. Or even a small one. I was in a town in the Arctic Circle. Conveniences I had taken for granted in urban areas were nowhere to be found. I would have to wait inside the station.

I went up to the door and pushed to open it. It wouldn't budge. I tried the door next to it. Nothing.

I rushed to look through the window, cupping my hands against it to shut out the sun. The lights inside were out. There wasn't a soul to be found. Fearing the worst, I quickly scanned the information on the doors.

The station was closed until morning.

Having come from Spain and not anticipating time outside in the cold, I was ill-prepared. Actually, I wasn't prepared at all. Like the misguided tourists on Ocean Beach, I didn't have a coat or hat or gloves. What was I going to do for the next six hours?

I wasn't the only one asking myself that question.

Matilda was from Vancouver, Canada. A short, attractive woman in her early forties, she had the body of someone who stays reasonably fit without much effort. Her round face was framed by long brown hair, and she had clear, kind eyes. A visual artist, Matilda was curious and engaging. When she asked a question or considered a response—including her own—she gave it genuine thought. She always seemed to look below the surface for meaning and nuance.

What she was looking for now—like me—was a hotel. The town only had a few. The ones we found were either closed for the night (they didn't get a lot of late-night walk-ins) or way too expensive. I was a high-school student on a shoestring budget. Matilda was a "starving artist" with her own budgetary limitations.

No place else to go, we turned to head back to the station. The sun was shining. The sky was a bright blue. The town was fast asleep.

As I had noticed at other stops on our way north, at the station drunk men slept on benches, overturned bottles beneath them. One snored. A couple of young guys at the other end of the platform appeared to be in the same situation as we were. Backpacks on the ground, the men loitered about, trying to pass the time.

Matilda and I did the same, trading anecdotes from our respective travels. She was visiting places throughout Europe, frequently staying in monasteries. I didn't even know that was possible, and I found it an intriguing way to travel.

The brutal cold meant we had to keep moving to try and stay warm. But after a long day on the road, we were both tired. We didn't want to keep moving. We wanted to get some rest.

Leaving behind the station a second time, we hoped to have better luck than on our first foray. Rather than go back into the center, where we were unlikely to make any new discoveries, we decided to survey the edge of town.

When we came upon a shut-down 4-H petting zoo, something caught our eye. Matilda and I both saw it at the same time. We looked at each other, posing the same unspoken question: should we do it?

We walked up to the structure. It was the quintessential chicken coop: a large wooden enclosure, low to the ground, with a plank up to a square entrance. It was painted brick red. It was full of hay.

But no chickens.

Chilled to the bone, the only thing either of us cared about was the possibility of some degree of shelter from the cold.

Like a fox about to raid a henhouse, Matilda got down on all fours and climbed into the coop. I followed.

It wasn't the Ritz. But neither was it nearly as bad as it could have been. Whereas I would have expected it to be filled with excrement, the hay seemed relatively fresh. There was no fowl odor. And there was no question that being inside the coop was better than being on the platform, exposed to the elements.

We lay down, heads on our backpacks. Circumstances notwithstanding, it felt good to stretch out. I was surprised to see a bee buzzing about. I hoped it was alone.

I came close, but never fell asleep. When we heard a voice outside the coop, however, both Matilda and I were jolted wide awake.

Without making a sound, we crept over to the edge of the entrance and peered around it.

A large penis was pointed in our direction.

Neither of us had expected to see a penis, regardless of its size. Yet there it was, in plain sight, just a stone's throw away. A steady stream of urine arched through the air, glistening in the sunlight as it fell to the earth. The urine was crystal-clear, provoking in me both admiration and envy.

And just so I'm clear, what I was feeling wasn't penis envy; it was pee envy. The young man was doing an incredible job of keeping himself hydrated. When I had urinated earlier, I had been disappointed and even a little ashamed to discover my own pee was dark yellow. If I'm being completely honest, it was practically a rust color. Just because I was traveling was no excuse not to drink enough fluids. I could do better—much better, in fact. If I had learned anything from the guy standing before me with exposed genitalia, it was that.

Matilda and I burst into muffled laughter, pulling away from the door, so we wouldn't give ourselves away.

The sound of pee splattering on the frozen ground stopped. Then, like an engine sputtering to a halt, it briefly started and stopped a couple of more times. Silence followed. It was short-lived, shattered by the sudden, unnerving smack of a rock against the exterior of our shelter.

We had been discovered. Apparently the young man—one of the guys we had seen earlier, stranded like us—had heard us laughing.

At first we kept quiet, hoping he'd think he was mistaken and go back to the station. Instead, he threw another rock. When we still didn't stir, he threw another. He knew someone was in the coop, and he was hell-bent on ratting them—us—out.

"Hello! Hello!" called Matilda.

Taking matters into her own hands, she scrambled out—again on all fours—to meet with our well-endowed assailant.

Matilda explained to the angry young man that we hadn't been laughing at his penis, but rather at the circumstances. On the contrary, she insisted, he had a penis of which he should be proud. Having seen no small number of them, she could say with some authority that his was an exemplary member.

After some additional back and forth with Matilda, the accidental exhibitionist headed back to his friends. I could have sworn he had a newfound strut in his step.

Matilda and I settled back down into our nests of straw. Giddy not only from the unlikely circumstances but from our surprise face-to-face encounter with the penis, we didn't get any sleep. We did, however, successfully avoid any frostbitten limbs—and we caught the first train out of town later that morning, bound for Helsinki.

21 THE DUNES

I woke up in a gritty pool of sweat mixed with sand.

Peter may have been Australian, but he was no less wary than I of the giant spider we'd seen the night before. The size of a small rat, it had what appeared to be feathery antenna. Last we had seen it, it had scrambled up into the rafters over the communal bathrooms. So, despite being in the middle of the Moroccan desert and not having air-conditioning in our room, we had closed the only window and made sure there was no way the fugitive in the rafters could get through—never mind under—our door. By morning, the room was sweltering, and I felt as dehydrated as if I'd lost half my body weight.

The plan for the day was to hike to the top of the largest dune in the area. If we wanted to get there and back without being burned alive by the desert sun, we had to get an early start.

On my way back from the bathroom, I knocked on our two travel companions' door. Jason was a clean-cut American with short blond hair, a matching goatee, and a sturdy athletic build. Gary was an Australian with a dark scraggly beard that hadn't been trimmed in weeks. The ragged t-shirt and baggy shorts he wore probably hadn't been washed in almost as long. Jason and Gary had met up in Ouarzazate, a town on the eastern side

161

of the Atlas mountains, and had been traveling together ever since.

"Come in," answered Jason.

I opened the door, taken aback by what I saw. Gary was as pale as a ghost and drenched in sweat. Stripped down to his underwear, it seemed to take everything he had just to prop himself up in bed.

"Are you alright?" I asked.

"Oh sure, mate. Just got a case of the shits is all."

"Oh no, that sucks! I'm really sorry. I guess you're going to have to stay behind today?"

"He won't," Jason interjected. "I keep telling him we can do the climb tomorrow when he feels better, but he won't listen. I even offered to stay behind with him, but—"

"No way. To hell with it. I'm going with you guys and that's that. What if I die tomorrow? I don't want to die without having climbed Erg Chebbi—not after coming all this way and dealing with all the bullshit we had to deal with to get here!" he laughed.

He stood up to get ready, but suddenly had second thoughts.

"Actually, I think I need to head to the bathroom first."

He grabbed his roll of toilet paper and pushed me out of the way, making straight for the toilets across the hall.

"Is he going to be alright?" I asked Jason.

"I have no idea. But there's no way he should be hiking in the desert if he's got the runs."

"Well, it's his choice. Looks like it's going to be an interesting hike."

The sun was just coming up as we embarked upon our foray into the dunes, light and shadow at ever-changing odds in the undulations of the desert floor. The smaller dunes nearest us were darker than the larger ones further off. Tans, golds, and oranges, fiery reds. As the sun rose and our trek progressed, the sands would take on those and other colors, too, countless shades and hues.

In places the sand was rippled like the surface of a pond. In others it was littered with footprints of birds and animals now nowhere to be seen, most preferring the cool light of the moon to the scorching heat of the sun. As for our fellow humans, if anyone had been there the day before, the wind had effaced all traces of them.

Our own steps grew heavier with each we took. The sand gave way beneath our weight, hindering our gait and slowing our progress. It may have cooled overnight, but the desert floor was already warm, like embers that had never completely gone out.

The four of us wandered off on our own respective paths, the massive dune that was our destination looming overhead. The challenge the desert posed felt personal. Although at times the unforgiving landscape brought us together, inevitably it pushed us back apart. Each of us had to confront it on our own terms.

Occasionally the desert deceived us. From one side a dune might appear to show the way, only to drop off precipitously when we got to the top. When that happened, all we could do was turn around and look for another route.

The trek was hard enough for me, in good health. I couldn't imagine what it must have been like for Gary. Jason never strayed too far ahead of him, frequently looking over his shoulder to make sure his friend was doing alright.

Relieving himself before we left had taken the pressure off Gary's intestines. For a while. Now, not even halfway to the summit, the rumbling started again, weakening his entire body. Undeterred, he kept going, doing everything in his power to ignore the war being waged on his insides.

His indomitable resolve notwithstanding, he was fighting a losing battle.

"Don't look back!" he yelled.

"What?" asked Jason, turning to look and instantly regretting it.

Gary had dropped his pants.

"Don't look back! Just keep walking! I've got to go!"

As much as he abhorred the idea of defecating in the dunes, Gary had no choice.

"What's up?" Peter shouted to Jason.

"He's got to go! Don't look back!"

I couldn't hear what they were saying, and turned to find Gary's tragic image far below. Amidst astonishingly beautiful, unsullied waves of sand, a lone figure squatted, holding a roll of toilet paper. It was a peculiar, paradoxical sight.

It was also a hilarious one. Knowing I was too far away to be seen or heard, much like Gary himself, I couldn't hold back. I burst into laughter, my own sides soon hurting almost as badly as his.

I was the first to arrive at the base of the biggest dune. Although I should have been covered in sweat, as I paused to catch my breath, I realized that in the dry heat my perspiration was evaporating as soon as it surfaced on my skin. Reminded of the need to stay hydrated, I took out my water bottle and looked behind me. Peter and Jason were both scaling the dune below, and Gary was on another not far behind.

I turned my attention back to my own ascent. A sheer wall of sand rising up before me, there was no easy way to the top. I would have to climb on all fours until I got to the lower end of the spine, which I could then follow up to the summit.

After another drink of water, I began scrambling toward the top. I didn't look up. I didn't want to know how far I had left to go. Instead, I concentrated on repeating my movements with as much economy as possible, my hands and feet sinking deep into the unstable sand over and over again. It was tough going, but I continued climbing, knowing that as long as I kept at it, I'd be to the crest in no time.

When I finally made it, I was astonished by what I saw. The smooth line demarcating where one side of the dune ended and the other began was extraordinarily precise. I didn't want to touch it. It pained me to think of defiling such perfection. I thought of the Buddhist monks who spend days meticulously rendering their sand mandalas, only to wipe them away in a dramatic testimony to impermanence. Sadly, if I wanted to see what was on the other side, I had no choice. I hoisted my weary body onto the spine, consoling myself that by morning the wind would erase all signs of my having been there.

One leg over each side of the crest, the soft sand now comforting ally as opposed to challenging adversary, I beheld an expanse of dunes so vast it defied the imagination. Calling it a "sea of sand" no longer seemed cliché; that was exactly what it was, its massive, successive golden waves rolling for as far as the eye could see.

When I got up to follow the spine to the summit, I looked down again at my friends.

"Almost there!" I hollered to Peter.

Jason was just behind him, but Gary had lost a lot of ground. I hoped we hadn't made a mistake by letting him come along.

The spine gradually sloped up toward the highest point of the dune. My walk felt like a victory march, and I savored each step as I continued to contemplate the staggering beauty visible in all directions. Even the bright blue sky was one of the most enthralling I had ever seen.

Peter joined me on the summit not long after.

"Wow," he said, taking a seat. "It's just incredible."

I turned to check on the others. Jason was just arriving at the crest a short distance below. Gary, on the other hand, had once again been waylaid.

"Uh oh, better just keep looking forward guys."

"Again?" asked Jason, his voice pained.

"No way!" Peter exclaimed.

Like witnesses to a train wreck, we couldn't help but look. It was every bit as tragic this time as it had been the first.

"The poor guy," said Peter.

"I told him not to come, I told him …" Jason lamented.

But then, out of nowhere, a laugh escaped him. He hadn't seen it coming. He hadn't laughed before. Now though, seeing it all again, the vulgar anomaly in such stark contrast with the breathtaking beauty, the irony was too much, the vision too absurd. He couldn't help it.

Having essentially given voice to something Peter and I were thinking but too afraid to say, all three of us burst into laughter. My eyes were soon so full of tears I could no longer see out of them.

By the time we stopped, Gary had regained enough strength to begin the final ascent. Somehow he had come this far, and nothing was going to stop him from making it all the way to the top.

I just hoped we didn't to have to bury him there.

While we took in the spectacular panorama, slowly but surely Gary pushed himself higher and higher. Eventually, having given it everything he had, he threw one hand over the dune's spine, followed by the other. Then, with one final, decisive heave, he pulled his head over it, too.

Peter, Jason, and I all looked over in response to the grunt heralding Gary's arrival. His pathetic image even more comical than before, we all broke into another wave of laughter, rushing over to help him make the final jaunt to the summit.

There was no need to ask how he was feeling. He looked like someone who'd been stranded on a desert island for years. He was even thinner than when we had met two days before and as pale as a corpse, the hair both on top of his head and in his beard matted with an unsightly paste of sand and sweat. He was not in good shape.

But he had made it.

Once we finished celebrating Gary's arrival and calmed back down, we all fell silent. Even someone hopelessly out of touch with their feelings or woefully lacking any sense of something greater would have been hard-pressed not to feel a profound reverence. For creation. For our place in it. For its humbling, awe-inspiring mystery.

22 RISING SIGN

I'd never had so much house to myself. Ever.

It was the kind of house that, under ordinary circumstances, I never would have been able to afford. But it was the off-season in Malta. And the house was in a very out-of-the-way place. The owners were glad to have anyone there at all; hence a price that had put it within my reach.

I had taken a two-hour bus ride from Valletta. Once I arrived at the northern tip of the island, I'd waited for my ship. When it came in, I climbed on board and found a place on deck. I wanted to be outside for the entire crossing from Malta to Gozo—already in sight even before we set sail.

After forty-five minutes of blinding sun and whipping wind, my skin a little darker, my crow's feet a little deeper, the taste of sea salt coating my lips, I swapped the boat for a bus. Eventually it dropped me in the village. From there, I made the long walk past the old church, down the steep hill, and into the wide-open Mediterranean countryside. A dusty breeze smelled faintly of manure. Once again, I was exposed to the sun.

I recognized the house from the photos online. It was impossible to miss, a small citadel perched atop a hill that it shared with just one other home. The walls enclosing it were stone, the same tawny shades that predominated throughout the dry, rocky landscape. A proliferation of prickly pears had claimed one corner of the small compound, and a lone tree shot up near the front door, which looked solid but was severely weathered. Some flowering vines tumbled over the wall next to it.

Inside, the house was a maze, a living, breathing structure that appeared to have organically taken shape over generations. There were so many rooms laid out with so little discernible logic, it would be days before I stopped mistaking other bedrooms for my own. Over and over I opened the wrong door, each time as baffled by my confusion as I was amused by its stubborn persistence.

Just as odd was the fact that the house had no interior stairs. In addition to the bedrooms, on the upper floor there was an atrium with huge windows that looked out over rolling hills, all the way to the sea. To go down to the massive kitchen or any of the other rooms on the ground floor, I had to venture outside, take an external flight of steps, and go back inside again.

In the enclosure behind the house, there was a neglected garden, its centerpiece a wise old carob with a thick, gnarled trunk. Its dense, dark-green canopy took to the sky like joy leaping from the heart, a relentless push and pull between harmony and chaos constantly redefining its ever-evolving form. Chocolate-brown seed pods littered the ground at its feet, fated to be squandered, like missed opportunities. In contrast, I would take full advantage of the carob's shadow, spending countless hours there searching for the right words.

A few days into my stay, I left my journal on the little metal table under the tree, and went inside to pee. There was a bathroom just off the kitchen.

The door was closed. When I opened it, I froze dead in my tracks.

On the other side of the room, I saw a huge scorpion. It reminded me of a lobster that had wandered in from the sea and, in a disoriented stupor, scaled the wall. It was frozen in place—no doubt plotting its next move. Or maybe instead, like a cat stuck in a tree, it was trying to figure out how to get back down, without breaking the neck it didn't actually have.

I cringed. The defenses protecting my hilltop fortification had been breached, my exquisite serenity obliterated by a threat I hadn't even known to anticipate. Suddenly I was back in Istanbul, reliving an experience from several years before.

I had returned to Turkey for a visit, and I was staying with friends. It was a hot summer night. The air was stuffy, my body was damp with sweat. I couldn't sleep, and I was parched, my throat sandpaper dry. I got up to get a glass of water.

As I walked down the dark hall, the cool tile felt good against my bare feet. Maybe rather than sweating in bed, I needed to be lying naked on the floor? Turks never wear shoes in the house. The floor was sure to be clean.

The kitchen was faintly illuminated by a street lamp on the other side of the window. I started to approach the sink. Something stopped me. I tried to dismiss my hesitation, but it was unwavering. My body would not budge.

I needed to turn on the light.

I did.

Like a booby trap left out in the open, a scorpion was lying in wait in the middle of the floor.

Between the fact that I'd never seen a scorpion, and the fact that I'd almost stepped on this one with my bare feet, I panicked. Did they move fast? Would it come at me, stinger pointed at my feet, claws targeting my toes? Or, potentially just as worrisome, would it scurry away before I had a chance to do something about it? And what would that something be? What was I supposed to do with Death incarnate loitering on the kitchen floor?

I had no idea.

I ran back upstairs and tapped on my friends' bedroom door, calling their names with hushed urgency. We didn't have a moment to lose.

"*Evet?*" came Doğan's sleepy voice.

"Ş*ey var?*" I exclaimed in my best Turkish. "Ş*ey var?*"

There's a thing!

Some mattress springs contracted and released. Feet shuffled toward the door. Doğan opened it, wearing nothing but briefs and slippers. His prematurely gray hair was tussled, his eyes so groggy I wasn't sure how long he'd be able to keep them open. If we didn't move fast, I feared he might fall back asleep standing. He followed me to the kitchen.

I pointed at the floor, anticipating Doğan's shock. The scorpion hadn't moved. Clearly, it didn't consider us a threat. Its massive pinchers, its poison-pricked tail, its impenetrable coat of armor—the scorpion had every reason to be confident in its defenses. What were we going to do? Seal off the kitchen? Call animal control? Evacuate?

Without missing a beat, Doğan took off his slipper, approached the unsuspecting arachnid, and smashed it like a bug.

That was, it turned out, all it was.

Oh.

It hadn't even occurred to me that a scorpion could be squashed like a mosquito or flattened like an ant. Given the scorpion's bad-ass reputation, it almost didn't seem fair. It was like the bubble-bursting moment when you realize a revered, larger-than-life idol is, in fact, only human. It reminded me of a clip I once saw where a highly respected judo master got knocked on his ass by a brutish mixed-martial-arts fighter. It took all of about ten seconds. The judo master didn't get back up. It seemed so wrong.

Before I could think of anything to say, Doğan smiled and headed back to bed.

Rather than waiting helpless in the middle of the floor, the scorpion I had just discovered was out of reach, high on the bathroom wall, almost to the ceiling. What's more, it was larger than the one in Istanbul. All I could imagine was the mess it would make, its guts splattering everywhere if I were to smash it.

Admittedly, though, the potential mess only partially explained my anxiety. Despite the lessons learned one hot summer night in Istanbul, I still hadn't overcome my fear of scorpions. I still considered them dangerous. When a friend on a flight from Mexico stuck his hand into his backpack, he felt what he described as a stake being driven into his finger. That was how he learned he had a scorpion stowaway.

Years later, when I was staying in an open-air, off-the-grid jungle hut south of Puerto Vallarta, I'd spent the entire week on the lookout for scorpions. Thankfully, I hadn't seen a single one. The day of my departure, sitting on the beach while waiting for my water taxi, I decided to confirm that my paranoia had been unwarranted.

"Ha!" the caretaker laughed. Oddly enough, he was a blond and blue-eyed twenty-something from Minnesota. "When the people in the hut next to yours were getting ready for bed, they found a scorpion under their pillow!"

Thank god no one had told me.

As for the Maltese mammoth now staring down at me from my bathroom ceiling, I suddenly had an epiphany. Why hadn't I thought of it sooner?

I stepped back outside and closed the door.

The eccentric old house was so large and had such a strange layout that I repeatedly became confused as I wandered through it. And it had multiple bathrooms.

The scorpion could stay.

The house was big enough for the two of us.

23 NO REFUGE

I discovered the Ardèche while searching for a way to stay in France and continue writing. A beautiful region northeast of Montpellier, it is known for its rolling pastures, forested mountains, and dramatic limestone gorges. More recently, the area had also become associated with the organic-farming, hemp-loving, gluten-free Bohemians who have settled there.

After a year on the road, my money was running low; but, I was making progress on my writing projects and enjoying my adventures. I had no desire to go home. I needed to get creative. I needed to explore my options.

Online I found a posting by a Welsh man named Danny. Danny had what he referred to as a "Creativity Refuge." He and his Irish partner, Helen, had purchased an abandoned farm in the Ardèche countryside. For the past year or two, they'd been renovating it. No small endeavor, they needed help.

A free spirit himself, Danny understood that creative types are often cash-strapped and in need of someplace to work. Why not come up with a win-win solution? He and Helen would provide room and board. Writers, artists, and musicians would provide labor in exchange for time and space to work on their own projects.

It sounded like a perfect setup. After all, I can only sit for so long before getting restless. I would write for a while, go tear down a wall or hammer some nails, and write some more.

I wrote to Danny. He explained his long-term vision that the Refuge serve as a repeat stopover for creative types passing through the area, a place for artists to rest, he said. A German woman who painted was arriving soon. Some other people had made inquiries, but no other guests were on the farm currently. I was more than welcome. And, there was so much to be done on the renovations, I'd be able to choose what I wanted to do. Danny emphasized that he had no expectations about what work or how much of it visitors did during their stays. I took that with a grain of salt, but I appreciated his laissez-faire attitude and his faith that others would make equitable contributions.

As for my own projects, Danny raved that the Refuge was a great place to write. It was large, with multiple buildings. I would have my pick of workspaces.

"And, of course," he made sure to mention not once, but two or three times, "there's always plenty of wine."

Of course?

We were in France. It was hardly a country known for wine shortages. Danny's assertion that it was a given there would be wine rang true; but, why did he feel the need to make it repeatedly? It was like insisting over and over that there'd be tapas in Spain, steak in Argentina, or sushi in Japan. It seemed odd.

A few weeks later, I hopped on a high-speed train from Paris, caught a couple of buses, and found myself at the closest town to the Refuge.

The town was a small, historic one, old buildings and narrow cobblestone streets branching out from the church in its center. I had arrived on a Sunday. Everything was closed. The sky struggled under the weight of thick, oppressive layers of gray and black. Alleys were slick from a dense mist saturating the air, and it was cool. When gusts turned tight passages into wind tunnels, it was cold. I was alone.

Until Danny showed up.

Danny had a lanky, medium-sized frame and mussed, wavy hair, dark brown with streaks of gray. His shirt untucked, his coat unzipped, he hustled around the corner to meet me. His gait was uneven, his efforts to exude a laid-back vibe somehow unconvincing. Artsy and upbeat on the surface, my gut said that deep down he was troubled. After apologizing for being late, he ushered me to his vehicle, which was illegally parked.

Something between a truck and a minivan, the vehicle was one of those curious, compact amalgams that's quintessentially European and rarely seen in the States. As we made introductory small talk, Danny piloted it out of town.

Soon we were traveling winding country roads surrounded by forest. As we began heading up into the mountains, however, the landscape began to open up. Ironic, perhaps, given that the fog got thicker and thicker, allowing me to see less and less. All the same, I caught glimpses of open pasture, often bordered by old stone walls. Occasional houses and barns were made of stone, too. The further we drove, the higher we went, the more remote it felt. There were almost no other cars. So much the better, since the fog became so dense it didn't seem safe to be driving. Danny didn't seem concerned.

"The German girl from Berlin arrives in a few days," he announced, referring to the painter he had mentioned in his email. "There's a German sculptor who might come, too, but he's not sure yet."

I looked forward to finding myself in a supportive community of artists.

Danny also volunteered that his partner, Helen, not only made the food with love, but that she had two children, both of whom were living at the Refuge.

"For now, anyway." He smirked. "Helen has a bit of a custody battle going on. And kids weren't supposed to be part of the deal down here, anyway."

I didn't press for details.

A single-lane country road eventually brought us to the farm. The fog was now so thick, it wasn't until we parked between the house and the barn that we could see either. The damp Earth exhaled life. Smoke was in the air. The atmosphere was somewhere between romantic and eerie.

We went inside, the door opening onto a dimly lit bedroom. It was part of a small annex adjoining the main house. A fire flickered inside a wood-burning stove.

"This is usually my room," Danny explained, "but you can sleep here if you want. Or, you can sleep up in the loft if you want a little more privacy."

In Danny's room I found a single bed, a nightstand, and an old armchair. The floor was covered with worn rugs, and some familiar contemporary-spirituality titles lined a couple of floor-to-ceiling bookshelves. Off to the side there was a room with a sink. I couldn't tell from where I was standing whether it also had a toilet.

The bedroom was fine. But before I made my decision, I wanted to see the loft, which was more akin to an attic space. I need a lot of alone time. Given that there was likely to be a lot of people at the Refuge, I found the prospect of more as opposed to less privacy appealing.

Danny motioned to the ladder. I started climbing.

"Oh my god!" I cried out, as soon as I reached eye-level with the upstairs floor.

Mere inches from my face was one of the largest spiders I'd ever seen. Looking me dead in the eyes, clearly it had been expecting me. The startling creature was perhaps half the size of the tarantula I'd once encountered in Sequoia. It was so large I'd had to stop my car to let it cross the road.

"There's a huge spider!"

I sounded ridiculous. I didn't care. A recovering arachnophobe, this took facing my fears way too literally. All I could imagine was the venomous beast jumping onto my nose and sinking its fangs into my eyes. Assuming I survived, I'd never see again. At least partial paralysis was probable, and there was a real danger of some degree of brain damage.

My hands gripping the ladder, I was utterly defenseless—and the spider knew it. So, unable to fight, I took flight. It happened so fast, I don't even remember scrambling back down.

"Yeah, there are a lot of those up there," Danny acknowledged.

"Down here looks good to me," I replied.

※

I still hadn't seen the bathroom.

When I asked, Danny clarified that, no, the room with the sink was not the bathroom. We walked over and stepped inside. There was a small refrigerator and a stove. It was a very basic kitchen.

The bathroom was on the other side of the bedroom, behind a closed door. Danny opened it, revealing a brightly colored shower curtain with a cartoonish underwater-world motif. Mermaids, seals, and seahorses frolicked amidst kelp, coral, and glittering sunken treasure.

I wondered if any of them noticed the peculiar smell.

It wasn't bad, per se. But neither was it good. It smelled like earth. Not the kind of earth in which you want to get your hands dirty. Not the kind of earth that gives off a fresh fragrance of renewal and vitality after a spring rain. It was a different, neither-good-nor-bad, hard-to-place sort of earth.

"We don't have plumbing yet," Danny explained, as I joined him in the bathroom. A toilet seat sat atop a plywood box. Danny raised the lid.

Earth, indeed. The toilet was full of dirt.

"So, we use this compost toilet. Have you ever used one before?"

Momentarily at a loss for words, I shook my head no. Had I overlooked something in Danny's emails about a lack of plumbing? And, were compost toilets usually kept inside the house, right off the bedroom?

"It's simple, really. You shit—the same way you usually do—and then you cover it up with a scoop or two of dirt, which is in here."

Danny lifted the lid on a full-size trash can, the kind used for yard waste. As promised, inside was more dirt. This dirt smelled better than the first. I could imagine gardening in this dirt. Perhaps that was because it wasn't yet mixed with human excrement?

"Once the bucket starts to fill up, we take it outside and dump it in back."

Danny had unwittingly made a great point. Truth be told, there wasn't a toilet. We were shitting in a bucket. Just because there was a place to sit did not make it a toilet.

I wondered what the pile out back looked like.

"There's no rush."

"It'll happen."

"Everyone contributes what and how much they want."

"There are no expectations."

Such was the philosophy of the Creativity Refuge, as it was described to me both prior to my stay and on the night of my arrival. Whether reluctant to give up his room or unable to stop pouring from the bottle, Danny sat on the floor near the fire and talked at me for hours. I sat on the bed, nodding politely. My neck grew tired, my eyelids heavy. I wondered how long I'd have to play host to my host.

In addition to his expectation-free approach to receiving guests, Danny shared his personal revelations on the power of intention, living in the present, and other life lessons that also happened to be espoused in the books on his shelves. He had been so taken by his spiritual heroes that he could regurgitate their teachings nearly verbatim. In principal, I shared many of his beliefs. In practice, it seemed a little odd to be discussing spirituality with someone slurring his speech.

By the time Danny left, I could barely keep my eyes open, never mind feign to pay attention to his New Age proselytizing. I knew the situation was dire when I found myself wondering if I shouldn't go live with the spiders, after all. Would Danny be less likely to seek me out if it meant having to go up and down a ladder while under the influence? Or, would he just sit at the base of the ladder, undeterred, spouting wisdom at me from below?

The next morning, I got up and headed to the shower. Before I turned on the water, though, I had to tend to other business. I had to complete another non-negotiable part of my morning routine.

I pulled up the lid and looked at the dirt. A couple of remnants of someone else's previous visits poked their heads through the soil, like decomposing slugs. Diverting my gaze, I tried not to inhale. The smell wasn't awful, but I hadn't gotten used to it. I could just about guarantee I never would.

I sat down on the seat made for a toilet. It was one of those spongy kinds that sink a little under your body weight, making a noise akin to how a more cultivated whoopee cushion might sound. Like those insufferable sofas that swallow you whole, I'd always hated spongy toilet seats. They seemed dated and cheap.

No spare toilet seats in sight, I put the spongy one out of my mind. I then pretended I was on an actual toilet. Thankfully, my backside doesn't have eyes. It didn't know the difference. My body responded with its normal zeal for letting go of the past.

The digested remains of yesterday's meals didn't have far to fall. In place of the familiar splash—something I wouldn't even think to question ordinarily—came the faintest of stirrings in the dirt. It was barely audible.

Somehow the whole operation almost seemed more humane. Rather than dropped to certain death like a lobster into boiling water, my solid waste landed where it was ultimately destined to end up; it landed where the water would have eventually taken it: back to the earth. The end of my own cycle was but the start of its own.

Now I had to bury it.

I got off the pot, and took the lid off the soil. I scooped some up, and let it fall into the bucket-cum-toilet, aiming for my fresh feces.

I had the slightest impression of experiencing what a mother must feel as she contemplates her newborn child: a profound pride that it had come from me; an undeniable sense of accomplishment that I had born to fruition the unsightly, semi-solid miracle resting in the bucket below. I had made that.

By the same token, I felt somehow more connected to the truth. This time it hadn't been sanitized. It was on full display. There was no water coming between me and it, no protective layer of Poo-Pourri to mask its noxious odor. I was forced to look it in the eyes (or were those kernels of corn?). This, too, was part of what I was.

Or, at least it had been, until I'd shat it out moments before.

The first scoop of dirt wasn't enough. I got another from the bucket.

My aim was better this time.

There was no rush. All the same, there was no time like the present.

Danny knocked on the bedroom door. Inviting himself into my mini-kitchen to watch me eat breakfast—standing at the counter, since the room wasn't big enough for a table—he made a perfunctory inquiry into how well I'd slept. He then turned the conversation to the real reason for his visit: a discussion about which renovation project I'd be working on.

The room originally used for baking bread was downstairs. I was instantly enamored of the space, the old brick oven, the stone walls, the vaulted ceiling. It had the feel of one of the old *caves*, or wine cellars, that Parisians are so fond of turning into underground clubs. The difference was that, although built into the hillside, in front the room had two windows with views of open pasture and rolling hills. It would make a great place to write.

All I had to do first was remove hundreds of years of soot, dust, and mold from the walls and ceiling.

It would be my first renovation project. And, it would consist of two phases: power-washing all the surfaces to loosen up the calcified grime, followed by chipping off every inch of it with a hammer.

Before I knew it, Danny had outfitted me with only slightly less protection than a hazmat suit. Waterproof overalls. Rubber gloves. Boots. Most importantly, a mask to prevent me from inhaling dust. Who knew what lay hidden in layer after layer of the centuries of build-up? Like ancient bacteria about to be released by a thawing Arctic, there was no telling what mysterious microorganisms I might be setting free. What I did know was that I didn't want to inhale them.

At first it was sort of fun. I'd never used a pressure cleaner, and the power was impressive, even exciting. It was like wielding a flame thrower blasting water instead of fire. Water ricocheted back at me off the walls and ceiling, bringing dirt along with it. Soon I was covered in both, as well as my own sweat. It wasn't long before my shoulders, arms, and back began to tire, but I liked the challenge. I enjoyed the physical nature of the work. I found satisfaction in progress so tangible and immediate.

After a few hours, the project off to a great start and my body weary, I decided to switch things up. I shed my work gear and headed to my room. Once I showered off the filth, it was time for some writing.

Danny and Helen came and went, also hard at work. I heard them outside my doors, both the one to the main house and the one to the outside. I stopped what I was doing when they flew through my room, repeatedly, their reasons never quite clear. Rather than left alone to do my own thing, I felt caught up in their frenzy, in the middle of everything. At times I even felt in the way. Concentrating was a futile struggle.

I also felt guilty. Despite having spent all morning pressure-cleaning, I felt uncomfortable working on my writing when

Danny and Helen were working around the house.

I knew it was silly. I knew my guilt was unwarranted. Yet the next couple of days, I faced the same struggle. Despite spending hours pressure-cleaning a dark, cavernous room where I could barely breathe, sweating like a pig and, when all was said and done, looking like one that had been rolling around in sludge, if Danny and Helen were working, I didn't feel right writing.

Perhaps that was because that's exactly how they wanted me to feel. Perhaps that was because not a moment went by during which I wasn't made aware not only of their presence, but of their tireless labor.

It wasn't a coincidence. It was a message.

And I got it.

I changed my approach. Rather than alternate over the course of the day between working for Danny and Helen and spending time on my own projects, I would dedicate my days to pressure-cleaning and my nights to writing.

My new plan was well-intentioned. It was also severely flawed. Pressure-cleaning was hard work. By the end of an afternoon of it, I was in no condition to write. Not only was my body exhausted, my fingers were spent from hours of gripping. I could hardly type. No less of a concern was Danny's need for someone to talk at each night, over a few glasses of wine. I wasn't going to accomplish anything while he was there. I'd probably be driven to excessive drink myself. Something else had to change.

Danny agreed.

One morning he pulled me into the downstairs room. I assumed he wanted to discuss my progress. I was caught off guard when, instead, he called into question my "vision" for the space.

My vision? Other than clean walls and a writing desk? For a room in his house, where I was merely a short-term guest? It felt like being asked to drink a saccharine-sweet glass of corporate Kool-Aid; it had the same bad taste of indoctrination. It made my stomach turn in the exact same way. Be a team player! Take ownership! Lead by example! Know your place, don't take your vacation, and no hard feelings when you're dead to us in the next downturn! I was on a farm shitting in a bucket doing slave labor for free—at the unintended expense of my own projects. Expecting me to have a "vision" for the room seemed a little over-the-top. I wasn't sure how to respond.

It didn't matter. Discussing my vision for the room wasn't the real reason we were downstairs.

Although he came at it from every angle except head-on, eventually Danny got around to telling me that he and Helen had been disappointed the day before, when I hadn't continued working after the pressure-washing was complete. They had expected me to start hammering away at the soot that evening, without delay. No matter that they hadn't told me.

I felt like a child who had just been reprimanded.

I was also very confused.

Over and over Danny had insisted there were no expectations. He prided himself on it, his love-and-light-filled approach to communal living. When had that changed? I had only been there a few days, after all. What about visitors contributing as much or as little as they felt compelled to contribute? And, by the way, almost all I had done since arriving was contribute. I had been busting my ass, in exchange for precious little of the promised time to work on my own projects.

Yet now I was being told I had let them down?

It didn't feel right. Not right at all.

Ute the German painter agreed.

She arrived the next day. And she was pissed.

"I don't understand," I overheard, as she and Danny got out of the van. "You said there was a studio space."

My bedroom door flew open. A big-boned, blonde woman in her late twenties stepped inside, throwing down a pile of bags. Danny was not far behind.

Ute may have been upset, but it wasn't with me. Her expression softened when she realized I was there.

"Matthew this is Ute. Ute is an artist from Berlin. Ute this is Matthew, a writer from San Francisco."

I wasn't sure whether to do the two kisses or shake hands. Ute didn't move. We settled for a respectful nod.

"You'll be staying up there," Danny said, pointing to the ladder.

If Ute heard my gasp, she didn't show it. Was Danny really going to make her stay in the loft? The baby-tarantula den? He had readily admitted my sighting wasn't a one-off, chance encounter. There were "lots of them up there."

Ute started climbing. I couldn't believe it was happening. I wanted to scream for her to stop, to let her know what unspeakable horrors awaited her. But it wasn't my home. It didn't feel right to contradict Danny in his own. And maybe Ute didn't care about spiders. Maybe I was a wuss, and Ute would dismiss my concerns as nonsense. Maybe she wouldn't even see any of the giant, hairy predators hidden in the rafters, behind the furniture, or under her pillow.

I hated myself for it, but I kept quiet. Ute seemed like a robust woman. Surely she could withstand a couple of spider bites? Several, even? From head to toe? And hopefully, if, say, she happened to end up wrapped in a soft cocoon of spider silk, she'd sleep that much more soundly, any ensuing loss of blood as benign as a blood-bank donation?

Hopefully.

The food may have been made with love, but dinner that night was anything but lovely.

Perhaps if there had been more of it, there would have been less conversation. Perhaps if, rather than love, rather than the freshest but most insubstantial of vegetable matter, the food had consisted of calories, of a little protein and maybe even some fat, tempers might have been tempered. Edible flowers are lovely, after all, but they're not very filling. Ute had little to distract her from the disturbing discoveries made upon her arrival.

"But you said I would have a place to work, and now that I'm here, you tell me there isn't anyplace."

We were in the main house, gathered around the dining table just off the kitchen. The grassy hill behind the farm was visible through a large window. The door to what I guessed was the living room was closed, and wherever there was a spare surface, piles of things—clothes, books, miscellaneous boxes—had taken over. Helen's little boy and girl were seated with us, by far the nicest—and sanest—of the bunch. Someone looking in from outside might have mistaken us for one big happy family.

"Things here are evolving," Danny began, sounding like a failed used-car salesman, as he digressed into a misguided, unconvincing attempt to put a positive spin on the situation. The way he told it, he was giving Ute the enviable opportunity of playing a hands-on role in creating her promised studio space. All it would take was a month or two of cleaning out a cold, wet, dilapidated old barn. Assuming none of the roof collapsed and she didn't catch pneumonia or get bit by a bat, the possibilities were endless.

Listening to Danny as I chewed my salad twice as long as usual, in the hopes of tricking my body into thinking I was feeding it twice as much food as I actually was, I was gripped by an overpowering sense of déjà vu. In hindsight, it was just as likely the moment my stomach starting feeding on itself.

As for Ute, Danny's attempt to instill in her a "vision" for a studio in the barn had fallen on deaf ears, ears out of which smoke was again billowing.

"I sent my art supplies from Berlin. I came all this way. But you weren't honest. I expected to do a work trade. I did not expect to build a studio from the ground up in a barn exposed to the elements."

"More bread?" asked Helen.

It was made with love.

The weekly farmers market was the next day.

Danny, Ute, and I piled into the van. As we pulled out of the driveway, the sun was shining, the sky a perfect blue. I admired the moss-covered rock from which not only the house and barn were built, but the walls running along the perimeters of the property. Heading down the mountain, I beheld lush pastures that gave way to a breathtaking succession of mountain ridges. I spied an ultra-modern windmill towering into the sky, out of place in rustic countryside that, otherwise, seemed lost in its own particular, immutable time.

We were almost to town when we made an unannounced stop at a gas station.

Danny turned off the engine. Pausing expectantly, he stared intensely ahead. He didn't say a word. Ute and I exchanged confused looks. Was Danny OK? I followed his line of sight. The only thing of note was a dumpster on the edge of the gas station lot. I turned back to Danny. He still wasn't moving, his eyes locked in the same stare, straight ahead. Had he entered some sort of mystical state? Perhaps he saw something that Ute and I could not?

I looked back at the dumpster, scanning it more closely this time, half-expecting to see something miraculous, one of those apparitions of the Virgin Mary, perhaps, her blessed tears streaming down the side of the big metal container.

But there was no Virgin Mary.

Danny was just waiting for us to get the hint.

Except for when he had picked us up initially, we hadn't gone anywhere in Danny and Helen's vehicles. What's more, not only were we their guests but, like the one meal a day, a weekly trip to the farmers market was part of the deal.

None of that mattered. Danny wasn't getting out of the van until we offered to pitch in for gas. Neither was he going to ask. He wasn't going to acknowledge that it was expected of us, since that would contradict his insistent, repeated claims he had no expectations. Instead, he wanted us to volunteer the money. If we volunteered, Danny would be above reproach—at least insofar as passive-aggressive coercion is irreproachable.

Opening my wallet, all I found was a twenty-euro note. No matter. Danny could give me change after he paid.

Danny snatched the cash like someone who doesn't trust their luck. I almost feared for my fingers.

He got out of the van without acknowledging the money.

While we waited, Ute and I made small talk. It wasn't long before she cut to the chase.

"So, what do you think of this place?" she asked, lowering her voice.

"Ah, well, I guess it's OK," I hesitated, uncomfortable having the conversation with Danny pumping gas just outside. "I mean, I'm still trying to figure it out."

"It's totally fucked up," Ute declared, leaving it at that since Danny had finished.

He got in, started the van, and we were off.

Much like the omitted thanks a few minutes earlier, Danny didn't offer me any change. I waited, thinking he'd bring it up once we were on the road.

He didn't.

Should I ask him for it? He was obviously going to give me some change, right? Gas was more expensive in Europe than in the States, but was it really that much more expensive? I didn't want to appear ungrateful, but twenty euros for a twenty-minute ride seemed exorbitant. Particularly when Ute had contributed as well. Particularly when we shouldn't actually be paying anything at all. Yet again, it didn't seem right.

Perhaps, on the other hand, Ute was.

The town was situated on a large river and surrounded by forested hills. Its main square was dominated by a picturesque medieval palace, complete with two round towers topped with steeply pitched roofs. Packed with animated vendors and eager townspeople, today the square was also covered in white tents. The market took place every week, but the atmosphere had a novel, celebratory feel.

We had come to the market to stock up on our personal provisions. Helen served the food made with love once a day. The rest of the time, Ute and I were expected to fend for ourselves.

Given that the food arrangement was so straightforward, Danny's last words before we each went off on our own caught me off guard.

"I'm sure Helen would appreciate it, if you showed your gratitude by buying some things for her kitchen."

Presented as a suggestion, it felt like a threat.

His tone. His energy. The way he drew close, springing the suggestion—the warning—on me out of the blue. I had a visceral reaction, my gut burning and my body trembling slightly, as though in danger. The interaction was brief, but it was meaningful. It felt dark and dishonest.

Danny disappeared before I had a chance to recover. Once again, I found myself in the uncomfortable position of trying to figure out his true expectations. Buy something? Or rather, "some things?" To show my gratitude? Like what? And how much? There was no shortage of options at the market. But, I knew neither what Helen might already have nor what she might need or want.

If I didn't know any of that, it was because the kitchen wasn't a communal one. I'd never cooked so much as an egg there—Ute and I weren't welcome in the main house, except when invited in by Danny or Helen. We had our own mini-kitchen, just downwind from the compost toilet. And, again, the deal—their offer—was that they would provide one meal a day. Yet now I was being told I had to contribute to that one meager meal?

As an offer of gratitude, no less.

Once again, like when I was reprimanded downstairs or said nothing after the gas-station petty theft, I played along.

But it wasn't because I was oblivious. It was no longer because I was trying to make sense of the situation, or was somehow OK with it. It was because I was under their roof, in the middle of nowhere, without any transportation. Short of fleeing on foot, I was dependent on them. I needed to play by their rules.

But only until I had made other plans.

I would be leaving as soon as I did.

The next day was no less full of surprises than the ones preceding it.

"Matthew," Danny began, pulling me into the main house shortly after I had awakened. Helen was there. Her little boy and girl were there. Everyone was seated around the dining table, all eyes expectantly on me. I understood right away. I had been called to an emergency meeting, already in progress.

"Ute is leaving. We've got to take her to the bus station," Danny announced.

"Oh? Really? She's leaving? That's weird. She didn't even tell me."

It was hardly a surprise that Ute would decide to go. But it seemed odd she hadn't mentioned it. We were practically living in the same room.

"She doesn't know yet," Helen volunteered, gripping her coffee cup, her knuckles bone-white.

"Doesn't know? What do you mean?"

It took me a second. Then I got it.

They were kicking her out.

"Her energy just isn't right for the Refuge. It's not working," Danny explained, as though still trying to justify it to himself.

"Oh, yeah," I replied. No one was going to argue with that. No one would mistake what Ute and Danny shared for chemistry. Maybe if he hadn't lied to her before she came to the farm? Maybe if he hadn't continued bullshitting her after she arrived?

"So, if you could be ready, in a little while, we'll be heading down to town."

"Oh. OK, sure."

Danny followed me to my room. Helen rushed the kids to safekeeping. The last thing we needed was for the youngsters to be taken hostage by a disgruntled German artist being evicted with no notice. It wouldn't be fair to drag the kids into this.

"Ute," Danny called up to the loft.

"Yes?" Her sleepy head peered over the ladder. Was that a spider on her shoulder?

"I'm sorry, but this isn't working out. I don't think we're a match. We're going to have to ask you to leave. In a little while, we'll be taking you to the bus station. Please gather your things, and get ready to go."

I didn't hear much of the ensuing conversation. Rather than bear witness to Ute's rage or, worse still, listen to Danny's self-righteous attempts to discredit it, I stepped outside for some fresh air.

Danny and Ute drove to town in the van. Helen, the kids, and I rode in the car.

The mood was somber at the bus station. Ute was no less incensed now than she had been at the farm.

"Love and light, Danny? Really?" she chastised, referring to how he always ended his emails. "This is your idea of community? This is your idea of treating people with respect? You're a liar. You wasted my time, and you've cost me a lot of money."

Danny said nothing. He was in the right. Ute was a raving lunatic who didn't understand he had taken the high road, that asking her to leave was in everyone's best interest. There was no point in engaging any further, since the ordeal was almost over. And he was coming out on top. Once she was gone, Ute would be forgotten. Things at the Refuge would go right back to normal.

It was almost as if he'd been through it all before.

As I watched Ute take her things out of the van, it hit me: I wasn't an innocent bystander. I, too, was playing a role in the unfolding drama. I had been enlisted as a sort of accomplice, unwittingly drafted to give weight to the opposing team, to ensure Ute felt outnumbered. Why else did I need to be there? Caught up in the maelstrom, I had switched into crisis mode. Like a good soldier, I had played along without stopping to question it.

I felt bad. I felt naive, stupid for falling for Danny's manipulation yet again. Rather than help send Ute packing, I should have been joining her. And I might have, except I still didn't have anyplace to go. I was working on it. But I needed a little more time.

When we got back to the farm, Ute's art supplies were in a pile near the door. Hundreds of dollars of them. Apparently it was cheaper for her to leave them behind than to mail them to Berlin—or wherever it was she was headed next.

Given the mission of the Refuge, it might have been assumed that the supplies would be saved for future resident artists. Yet something told me that wasn't how it was going to play out. Something told me Ute's supplies would be up on eBay before the end of the day.

Several more days passed before I figured out my own plan B, each evening spent online exploring options and looking into logistics. In the meantime, I finished my renovation project. Hammer in hand, I chipped away every inch of build-up on the walls and ceiling, sending big, blackened, plaster-like chunks of soot, dust, and mold falling to the ground. It was grueling work. At the end of each session, I put the debris into large bags and carried them outside to the trash.

If I was still working on the project, it was no longer out of a feeling of obligation. I felt no need to keep my end of the bargain with my hosts. My hosts were liars, their bargain a scam. A deal with the Devil would have been more fair. Crazy though it might seem, I was finishing the room for my own satisfaction, for the sense of accomplishment that comes with taking on a challenge and seeing it through to the end.

I'd also developed an affection for the room itself. It was never going to be mine. I had managed to get a table into it, but, once again, opportunities to write were sporadic. Even when I had them, I didn't feel inspired. I was too agitated to throw myself into writing. I was ready to leave. As far as the project was concerned, though, none of that mattered. A plastic surgeon doesn't stop halfway through a facelift. I wasn't going to stop peeling back the layers of time on the room until every speck of black was an age-defying light-gray.

Continuing to work in the room was also a great pretext for limiting my interaction with Danny and Helen. There was, however, one crucial interaction I still had to have with them.

I decided to do it at dinner.

"Just wanted to let you know that, now that the room is done, I'm going to be moving on."

Danny and Helen said nothing, letting the news register.

"We're really sorry to hear that," Helen offered, her fork suspended in midair.

"Yeah, we thought you were going to be here at least another two weeks—you're only halfway into your first month," Danny remarked. He tried to sound concerned, maybe even a little hurt. In reality, he was pissed. The gullible visitor had figured him out?

"Being at the Refuge has been great, but I'm not getting any writing done. So, I think it's time to take off, so I can get back to that."

"But your room is finished."

My room.

Danny thought he was waving a carrot. He didn't get it. I now saw the situation for what it was. The ruse was over. His beta carotene had given me food poisoning.

"Yeah, I wanted to see it through to the end. Now that I have, it's time for me to head out."

"Well, OK," said Helen, tentatively. She shot Danny a look. "We sure have enjoyed having you here."

"Thanks, Helen. I've really appreciated your food made with love."

I meant it. The combination of low-cal meals and rigorous physical labor had resulted in considerable—and welcome—weight loss. After two weeks on the farm, I was beginning to have trouble keeping my pants up.

"When are you leaving?" asked Danny.

"Tomorrow, if you don't mind taking me to the bus station."

Danny swallowed hard. He had miscalculated. I really was going.

"Yeah, sure," he replied, clenching his jaw.

Another awkward silence followed. To do something, I picked up the pitcher and refilled my glass of water. It was filtered with love.

"Actually," Danny began, "if you want, I can give you a ride all the way to Grocon."

"Oh, really? Thanks. That's really nice of you."

The closest bus station—the one where we'd banished Ute into exile—was a half-hour drive. Grocon was about a forty-five-minute one. I appreciated Danny's willingness to take me a little further, which would cut one leg from my trip.

"It would just be, you know, like ten euros."

I should have known.

I had already given Danny gas money. Plenty of it. In fact, as far as I was concerned, I'd given him at least ten euros more than I should have—probably more like fifteen. Yet, rather than acknowledge the money I had already given him, he was trying to wrangle still more out of me? It was infuriating. And it wasn't going to happen. Not this time.

"Don't worry about it. I'm in no rush, and I don't want you to go out of your way."

"It's no trouble, really—"

"No, Danny," I interrupted. "I'd just like to go to the regular station. I'll get the bus to Grocon from there. Thanks again for your offer—I appreciate it. But I insist."

The next day, after I'd said quick goodbyes to Helen and the kids, Danny took me to the bus station. We made small talk in the van; or, rather, he did. I no longer had any reason to pretend to care. I participated enough to be polite, nodding and giving one-word indications that I was following along; but, mostly I just watched the scenery—the one and only thing I would miss from my time in the Ardèche.

When we got to the station, I jumped out of the van. Like an inmate released from a sentence of hard labor, I savored the taste of freedom for the first time in weeks.

I went up to the ticket counter to buy my ticket to Grocon. Six euros.

Post script:

Years after my misadventure in the Ardèche, my curiosity led me to do an online search for the Creativity Refuge (not the place's real name). What, I wondered, had become of it? Had Danny and Helen (not their real names either) managed to make their vision a reality? Had they learned from their mistakes with guests such as Ute and me (once I was at a safe distance, I had sent Danny a lengthy, detailed explanation of the true reasons for my departure, including suggestions for setting expectations with future guests)? Were they now offering a variety of programs? Were groups of artists, musicians, and writers stopping over at the rural retreat like flocks of geese touching down in autumn lakes and ponds?

My search produced no results. Apparently the Refuge was no more.

I wasn't surprised.

Upon completion of these stories, I tried again.

Bingo.

Stolen money. Sexual liaisons. And, for the grand finale, a police raid.

A blog had been set up by a woman who had gone to the Refuge a few years after my stay. The blog had several other contributors, as well, none of whom had anything good to say.

Danny had started charging for courses at the Refuge. When the courses were canceled, allegedly there were no refunds. Bloggers complained of being swindled out of thousands of dollars. When the courses did take place and Danny was attracted to one or more willing participants, he had sex with them. Attendees who hadn't signed up for an orgy reported that Danny's intrigues did little to foster a supportive, collaborative community.

Helen's name appeared nowhere in the blog posts. Assuming the allegations were true, my guess was that she either wised up or Danny sent her packing. Helen had been replaced by a woman named Kathy, who was shown as contact for the Refuge on an out-of-date web page. A picture of her lovingly fondling a ripe bunch of dark-red grapes spoke to the deep connection with the earth that could be made on the farm. Kathy's coquettish smile spoke to the fun that could had if you were up for sex with Danny.

That fun had long since come to an end.

Evidently the French authorities had taken the stories of a few cheated attendees very seriously; so seriously, in fact, that the police had raided the Refuge, shutting it down. According to a firsthand blog account, things had gotten so bad in the Refuge's final days that two females had fled on foot. Given that it was a thirty-minute drive to town, I could only guess how long it would have taken to walk—particularly since the women didn't follow the road. Presumably in the interest of their safety, the escapees instead made the long, unmarked trek over the bramble-covered mountain behind the farm. Hours later they eventually came to a road. From there, they hitchhiked to the nearest village.

I had no idea how lucky I was to get out when I did. I had lost some time, but no money. My interactions with Danny were bizarre, but I never felt a need to run for my life.

Never one to be down for long, after the Creativity Refuge was shuttered, Danny had mounted another alleged scam. He had become an antiques dealer; a dealer of antique French toilets, to be exact. It made perfect sense, given that he himself was so full of shit. He sold the toilets online, as I learned from yet another blog, this one dedicated to victims of that apparently fraudulent scheme.

According to his second (or third? or tenth?) group of self-proclaimed victims, Danny had repeatedly accepted money for antiques he failed to deliver. One story was long and detailed, complete with an email exchange with Danny in its entirety. I read every single line, relishing each and every word. I was sorry for Danny's latest victims. But I was fascinated to discover the unexpected afterward, riveted by his communications with the swindled would-be customer. It was all so familiar. The same voice. The same tactics. The same manipulation.

And the same outcome.

Whenever his customers reached the end of their patience with his convoluted lies and endless excuses, Danny turned on them. A victim of circumstance, he was a struggling artist, not in it for the money. They were insensitive greedy bastards intent on his ruin.

Poor guy.

Because his scams had involved multiple countries and crossed national borders, one blog claimed Interpol had gotten involved. And yet, as I write these words, a website for what is ostensibly Danny's latest endeavor is live—complete with festivals he will be attending throughout Europe this year as a vendor.

Not only is Danny still going, he isn't even hiding.

I hope his antics will finally catch up with him. I hope that one—or, better yet, several—of his victims are planning a trip to one of those festivals, Interpol in tow.

24 LET IT FLOW

I had enough experience to know what to expect on a Turkish bus.

Before I had boarded, like a plant struggling in the stifling heat, I'd questioned how much longer before I withered. Now I'd gone from one extreme to the other. The interior of the bus was subsumed in an arctic chill. Long-distance Turkish buses tended to overcompensate for the severe summer temperatures by subjecting their passengers to a wintery cold. Just like when American retailers and restaurants did the same thing, I hated it. How many times had I ended up with a splitting headache? Never mind my annoyance at such a decadent waste of energy.

My jacket—a sandy-colored suede one from the 70s, given to me by the great-uncle who had also given me his name—lay on the window seat next to me.

The bus pulled out of the station, and the trip got underway. Not including stops, the trip to Eskişehir was about a four-hour one.

Although we would pass through other urban areas, once we eventually left Istanbul behind and crossed into Anatolia— the name for the Asian part of Turkey—much of the trip took us through rural landscapes. Other than parched grasses and weathered rock, the hilly terrain was spartan for the most part. There weren't many trees, and there wasn't much water, with the notable exception of a huge freshwater lake whose shores we briefly followed.

Because of the heat, at the terminal I'd drunk a lot of water. I'd been conscious not to overdo it, since I was about to get on a long-distance bus. Still, I was sweating out the water almost as fast as I consumed it. Not drinking enough posed a greater risk than possibly drinking too much. I tried to find the right balance, sipping from the water bottle, as opposed to taking long gulps, and making sure I went to the bathroom before our departure.

My foresight helped. But there was never any chance I'd make it the entire trip without going to the bathroom. Drop by drop, like sands in an hour glass, fluid trickled from my kidneys to my bladder.

At first it wasn't that bad, and I easily put it out of my mind. As more and more scenery rolled by, however, a pressure began to build on my insides. Soon I was unable to ignore it. It was like needing to pee in the middle of the night, and realizing that—try and try as you might—you're never going to fall back asleep until you do.

I really had to go.

There wasn't a toilet on the bus. I knew from previous trips that we'd be stopping midway for a bathroom break. Based on how long we'd been traveling, that had to be sooner rather than later. I crossed my legs a little tighter, again trying not to think about it. Again, I failed. Miserably.

A half an hour later, we were still in the middle of nowhere. Nothing in the barren landscape suggested we were near any sort of civilization, nor had there been any road signs offering hope we'd be stopping anytime soon.

Meanwhile, pressure had turned to pain. My bladder was starting to hurt. The situation was no longer simply about needing to pee or even needing to do so badly. It was fast becoming about a potential medical emergency.

I didn't know what to do. Surely we'd be at a rest stop

shortly. We had to be. We'd already been traveling for more than two and a half hours.

But that wasn't the point.

The point was that I had to go. Now. Rest stop or no rest stop. My bladder had exceeded its capacity, and it was threatening to burst.

The pain became serious enough that I considered asking the driver to stop, so I could urinate on the side of the road. I could already anticipate his reaction: the self-important *Amerikalı* wanted his needs prioritized over those of everyone else on the bus. Just because he had to pee. He couldn't wait until the bus stopped, like the rest of the passengers, none of whom would even think of making such a shameless request. The driver, of course, would have no way of knowing I'd been on countless long-distance bus trips, and never once found myself in such dire straits. He'd just think I was an entitled, whiny pain in the ass who spoke really bad Turkish.

"Please, piss my making very necessary became!"

I couldn't do it.

But neither could I wait. Not for another moment. It was no longer an option. I had to go, and I had to go now.

I looked around. The bus wasn't very full, at least not in my immediate vicinity. The seats on the other side of the aisle were unoccupied. There was someone directly behind me, but the seat between them and the window was vacant, just like mine. There were people in the row in front of me, but I was less concerned about them. They were facing the other way.

I looked at my water bottle. It was almost empty. I looked at my jacket. It was still lying on the seat, unused.

That was about to change.

Looking around one more time to make sure the coast was clear, I picked up my water bottle and drank the last few gulps. Ironic, perhaps, given my dilemma. But I didn't want it to go to waste—and I needed the bottle.

I reached for my jacket, and spread it over my lap.

Was I really going to do this?

More important, could I really do this? Could I pull it off?

Never mind the logistics, what about the sound? It was a universal one, one the other passengers would instantly recognize. How could I hide it? The bus was poorly insulated from outside noise, but neither that nor the lively but feeble radio up front would come even close to drowning out what I was about to do.

A sharp, stabbing pain shot through my lower abdomen, the worst yet. I didn't have a choice.

Unfortunately, neither did I have a third hand.

I could have used two for the bottle alone, which required exact positioning. But there was also the writhing one-eyed monster himself, whom I had to align with the bottle opening, again with a precision leaving no margin for error. It was like trying to force-feed a cat its medicine, somehow holding its mouth open while also getting the pills down, more difficult still, given that I couldn't watch. I needed help. The entire operation, after all, had to be executed beneath my jacket— raising another issue. I needed yet another hand (I was now at four or five) to hold the jacket over the bottle; otherwise, I risked peeing on it.

My internal organs now on the verge of failure, their painful reminders increasingly frequent, each time more severe, I gave it a go.

I'd hoped to discover I'd been overthinking things, that my concerns had been exaggerated. Instead, they proved right on the mark: I didn't have enough hands. I got the bottle into what felt like the right position, but I struggled to keep the opening of my flaccid manhood aligned with it. Perhaps if it weren't flaccid? Maybe I needed to wake the sleeping beast? Even with the jacket over my lap, what that would require seemed sure to raise suspicions, if not get me thrown off the bus. Or beaten. Or jailed.

My jacket posed a real problem, too. I had to have it over my legs for privacy; but, like so many clingy shower curtains elsewhere on my travels, it kept getting in the way.

Challenges notwithstanding, I still had to pee.

I took a deep breath. I tried to relax. I willed the floodgates to open.

Apparently they were on lockdown.

Never in my life had I needed to urinate so badly. And yet, despite the ridiculous lengths to which I'd just gone so that I could, nothing came out.

I started to panic. But then I caught myself, again trying to relax. I was in real pain. I had to figure this out. I had to forget about the unusual circumstances. I had to think about flushing toilets and cascading waterfalls and dams breaking. I had to visualize myself alone in the middle of a pristine field, peeing for the sheer pleasure of it, for no other reason than because I could—making sure not to stand facing into the wind.

Without warning, the bus slowed and jerked to the side. I looked up.

A rest stop.

My bladder may have just refused to let out so much as a drop, but my eyes were suddenly moist with tears. Tears of joy. Tears that, oddly enough, smelled of the asparagus I'd eaten the night before.

I hoped that, in addition to toilets, a café, and a mini-mart, the little complex also included an organ-transplant facility. I found comfort in the fact that, not being in my own country, I might actually be able to afford the procedure.

The bus hadn't even come to a halt before I was on my feet. That's when I discovered I could barely walk.

My lower abdomen was an excruciating tangle of cramps so severe my bladder might have been hemorrhaging. Standing up was hard enough. Putting one foot in front of the other was unbearable. My abs, my back, my thighs, every muscle was as tight as a closed fist. The pain wasn't something I could just play off. There was no grinning and bearing it. Instead, I hobbled down the stairs in agony, as incapacitated as a frail ninety-year-old man. One of the first off the bus and the last to the restrooms, I was a turtle surrounded by hares, everyone whizzing by me on their way to empty their own overflowing bladders.

By the time I made it to the toilets, most of the first wave of passengers had come and gone. I went into a stall, for some privacy. I knew I was also going to need some time.

As foreshadowed by my frustrated attempt on the bus, after putting so much effort into holding back the deluge, my body couldn't just flip a switch and let it all come rushing out. Muscles had to relax. I had to breathe. My entire body had to get the message: it was OK to go now.

Finally, a couple of minutes later, in a dark, dirty stall at an anonymous roadside stop in Western Anatolia, I had the most satisfying, mind-blowing gusher of piss my body has ever known. The force was like the kickback of a revolver. The mighty stream flowed on and on. And on. Then it flowed some more. It flowed for so long I began to wonder when it would end. I almost started to fear being left behind, unable to pull myself away from the restroom, as the bus pulled away from the rest stop. If I'd been peeing into a toilet bowl instead of a dank hole in the ground, it might have overflowed. Yet even then, I would have been powerless before the unstoppable outpouring. As pressure had given way to unbearable pain, pain now gave way to delirious pleasure—I had experienced less satisfying orgasms. I feared being on the verge of one now, so sublime was the release, so exquisite the rush.

Having peed out half my body weight, I shuffled back to the bus. Whereas ordinarily I would have grabbed something to drink for the second leg of the trip, this time I didn't so much as glance at the mini-mart, never mind set foot in it.

I wasn't thirsty.

25 GRIN AND BURY IT

I dreamt about it before it happened.

That did not mean I knew how it would end.

It was Sunday evening at the country house I'd rented on the Spanish island of Mallorca. The jagged peaks of the mountains across the valley rose up imperiously, clawing at the sky as though calling to the sun, reminding it of their rendezvous. It was well on its way. Soon it would retreat behind them, en route to meeting other pressing obligations in distant lands, its work never done. I looked forward to its departure each night. More often than not, it put on a spectacular show.

The surroundings were alive with end-of-day activity. Songbirds fluttered and chirped in the rows of olive trees extending down the hill to the winding one-lane road. A pair of *put-puts*—curious, beautiful birds that looked like a cross between a roadrunner and a flicker—ambled about on the gravel driveway. They were regular visitors. A red kite briefly came and went, and the rat sat in its hole in the old stone wall. Like me, it was having dinner, unconcerned about my presence a safe distance away on the terrace. I wasn't concerned either. I didn't mind him in that wall; I was, however, perturbed that he and his friends had started running up and down the wall between my bedroom and the bathroom, repeatedly waking me up in the middle of the night. I prayed I wasn't going to find the beady-eyed rodents staring down at me one morning from a hole over my head.

I finished my meal and went inside. As I washed off my plate, water began backing up into the sink. The drain had been slow that morning; now it had stopped up completely. I hated using nasty chemicals, but I feared that tomorrow I'd be buying some Drano.

I stepped back outside and ran down the short flight of stairs from the terrace to the driveway. Pea gravel crunched under my feet, and rural aromas perfumed the air. Sweet almond blossoms. Mediterranean herbs. The rich vitality of the Earth itself, as it let out a deep sigh of relief after a long, hot day. Dogs barked in the distance, as usual.

The laundry machine was in the garage, under my bedroom. I had put in a load when I'd made the half-hour walk up from the village earlier. I hadn't timed it, but I assumed my clothes would be done by now.

The metal garage door, one of a pair, let out a sustained, tortured protest—making unpredictable, dramatic changes in tone—as I pushed it inward, clanging to a reverberating halt against an interior wall. I walked inside. Right away, something didn't feel right. With each step, my shoes made an unexpected noise. I looked down.

Water.

My eyes darted to the washing machine just a few feet away. Water had gathered around its base. I assumed it had overflowed. But then I followed the water, turning toward the back of the garage.

It was flooded. All of it.

I remembered the dream I'd had a few weeks earlier, before I knew I'd be renting the country house. Quite simply, I had dreamt I was staying in a house that flooded.

Dreams really do come true.

"Shit!" I said, fearing this dream had the makings of a nightmare.

Rushing to curtail potential losses, I scanned the garage for anything susceptible to water damage. I grabbed cardboard boxes sitting on the floor, running them outside without pausing to check their contents. I cringed when I discovered a few paintings up against the wall, grabbing them, too, quickly wiping off wet edges. I didn't have to worry about the wheelbarrow or garden tools or most of the other items in storage. I hoped I wasn't overlooking anything.

I caught my breath, finding some comfort in the fragrant air. I needed to let the property manager know what had happened. I went inside the house and got my cell phone; or, rather, the cell phone my German friend on the island had lent me for my stay. I texted the property manager in Palma, the island's biggest city, down on the coast. He responded right away. After apologizing for the inconvenience, he reminded me it was Sunday night. I was living in the country outside a small village. There wasn't anyone to call, not until tomorrow.

What was I going to do between now and then? I couldn't just let the water sit there, covering the garage floor. It was wastewater. Like a rotting corpse, it wouldn't be long before it began emitting the foulest of odors. Soon it could smell as bad as my shoes.

As destructive as it was life-giving, I feared the water might also do damage. Metal might begin turning to rust. Mold spores might discover the perfect conditions for an outbreak. Some other calamity might happen that I couldn't even anticipate.

And then there was my biggest concern: I could pee outside, but what about the other, messier physiological process? I knew my vegetarian body. It would have nonnegotiable needs long before the plumber showed up sometime the next day.

I went back down to the garage. The deeper into it I ventured, the deeper the water got. I watched my step, grateful for my water-resistant hiking shoes. The flooding was never more than an inch high.

In the far left corner, I found the source of the problem.

The pipes from the house and washing machine emptied into one that drained into the septic tank outside. That pipe was blocked. Insensitive to its struggle, the other two were still trying to send water down it. Like a foie gras duck that can't be force-fed another bite, anything else shoved down the pipe's throat was coming right back up.

And being vomited the length and width of the garage.

I had little firsthand experience dealing with plumbing issues. But I figured it couldn't be that difficult: if the pipe was blocked, I just needed to unblock it.

I recalled that plumbers had a device they stuck down clogged pipes, some sort of long wire that snaked into the plumbing and wrestled blockages out of the way. I didn't have that sort of apparatus, but I did have a garden hose. Maybe it was close enough to do the trick?

I went outside, got the hose, and brought it into the garage. Sticking it into the hole in the floor, it wasn't long before the end of the hose came into contact with the blockage. I moved the hose from side to side, and then in vigorous circles. I pushed it forward and pulled it back. I attempted other variations, moving the hose every which way.

Water lurched up, then dropped down, bubbling and gurgling, as though drowning in itself. The hose was clearly having some sort of effect, but the water was still there—the single, definitive flush I had hoped to instigate was not happening. Was any water at all making its way to the septic tank?

I ran outside, a short distance down the hill. With a forceful heave, I lifted the metal lid off the underground tank. I saw where the pipe from the house spewed wastewater into unseen depths. Ordinarily. In the dim light, now all I saw was a faint trickle. Was it progress? Or, had it been there before I began my efforts?

It occurred to me that turning on the hose might help. Perhaps water pressure at the source of the blockage would dislodge it, especially if there was already even the smallest of openings in the clog, a crack in its defenses waiting to be exploited. I needed to take advantage of it. I needed to blast the blockage out of the way and into septic oblivion.

I ran up to the spigot outside the garage. The hose was already attached to it. I turned on the water, and went back inside. Again, I moved the hose in circles. Again, I pulled it partway out, then shoved it back down, hoping to use it like a battering ram. Like before, the water responded with drops in level, giving me hope, followed by surges toward the surface that made me question whether I was making any progress. The water level then dropped again, though I could still see it. I decided to go back down to the tank, to see if the flow had increased.

The sky losing its earlier luster, I peered into the septic tank. A small stream trickled into the darkness, but it wasn't noticeably more significant than before.

I was disappointed. I felt defeated.

I'd done all I could. I couldn't think of anything else. I'd have to wait for the plumber.

Slowly making my way back up the yard, for the first time I felt how tired my body was. I'd been in panic mode since discovering the flood. The adrenaline rush finally petering out, only now could I begin to relax.

But then I stepped into the garage.

Not only was there more water than before, the water was filthy. The closer I got to the pipes, the worse it was. Semi-solid matter floated on the surface. Lots of it. I knew what it was, and I knew why it was there. I had forgotten to turn off the hose. I was flushing the deepest contents of the pipe up into the garage, bringing its darkest secrets to light.

I bolted outside to the spigot, turning it off with a single, forceful twist. The rat looked over at me, still chewing. He shared none of my concern.

The garage now full not only of water but raw sewage, I had no choice: I couldn't leave it overnight. If the rats didn't wake me up, the foul stench rising up from the garage surely would.

I got the mop and bucket from the kitchen and, with heavy

heart, again made my way down the stairs. This was not how I wanted to spend my evening. It didn't matter. We don't always get to choose. For the next hour and a half, I squeezed mop-full after mop-full of sullied water into the bucket. I lost count of how many buckets I filled.

I didn't have much left of my clean-up effort when I felt a familiar movement in my gut.

Oh shit.

It wasn't just the movement itself, but the specific nature of it. It was more than just a heads-up about a developing situation. It was a declaration of a need that would have to be addressed sooner rather than later.

I didn't even try to ignore it. Better now while there was still a little sunlight. I'd seen a pine marten on my roof a few nights earlier. Their faces looked like adorable little teddy bears but, as the rat could emphatically attest, they were known for being aggressive nighttime predators. The last thing I needed was for one to bite me in the ass.

I grabbed a roll of toilet paper from the bathroom. Stepping back outside onto the terrace, I considered my options. The front yard was private, shielded from the road by a fence and overgrown vegetation. Still, it didn't seem right.

I walked around the side of the house, up a steep slope. A nearly vertical mountainside rose up from the backyard, which was almost flush with the roof. The yard was small, overtaken in most places by tall grasses. A dilapidated shed was filled with junk. There were olive trees gone wild. There was absolute privacy.

The middle of the yard was mostly clear of trees, grasses, and debris. It was the most logical place for me to do the deed.

A few swallows circled overhead. I hesitated, though not because I'd have an audience after all. I still wasn't comfortable with the notion of defecating in my hosts' backyard. It was a far cry from shitting on someone's grave; but, still, it felt disrespectful. And what if they found out? What if they were somehow able to make the connection between the disturbed earth my hole would leave behind and the disaster in the garage?

My insides rumbled.

It didn't matter. I had to go. Now.

I found a garden shovel and dug a hole. I then dropped my shorts, squatted, and surrendered. My eyes wandered up and down the rock wall a short distance away. I breathed in the sweet smell of pine. Another cycle came to a predictable end. Like a good orgasm, this time was no less satisfying than those before it. I felt immediate, gratifying relief. I then wiped, pulled up my shorts, and filled the hole with dirt.

Doing my best to cover up any signs of the disturbed earth, I imagined my hosts nonetheless finding the hole and digging up its contents—before they'd left their guest review on AirBNB.

"Matthew was a wonderful guest. Unfortunately, he shat in our yard."

And yet what was done was done. The situation was now out of my hands.

I headed back to the terrace to witness the sun's final moments.

ABOUT THE AUTHOR

Matthew Félix is an author, podcast producer and host, and traveler. Adventure, humor, and spirituality infuse his work, which often draws on his time living in Spain, France, and Turkey, as well as travels in over fifty countries.

Matthew's debut novel, *A Voice Beyond Reason*, is the story of how a young Spaniard's awakening to his intuition gets him out of his head, so he can follow his heart. Matthew's travel-story collection, *With Open Arms*, recounts his humorous and harrowing experiences on two trips to Morocco. The award-winning collection has topped the Amazon Africa category, as well as the Morocco one three times.

Matthew's video podcast, *Matthew Félix On Air*, features guests discussing writing, travel, culture, and more. Matthew has also produced three podcasts based on his books.

In his free time, Matthew is likely to be found exploring the streets of San Francisco or hiking the trails of Northern California.

matthewfelix.com

CPSIA information can be obtained
at www.ICGtesting.com
Printed in the USA
LVHW011952180619
621611LV00013B/654/P